D1582789

Greenhill Books

OR GO DOWN
IN FLAME

OR GO DOWN IN FLAME

A Navigator's Death Over Schweinfurt

by

W. Raymond Wood

Greenhill Books, London

Published 1994 in the United Kingdom by
Greenhill Books, Lionel Leventhal Limited,
Park House, 1 Russell Gardens, London NW11 9NN

Copyright © 1993 by W. Raymond Wood

All rights reserved. No part of this book may be reproduced or
utilized in any form or by any means, electronic or mechanical,
including photocopying, recording or by any information
storage and retrieval system, without the written
permission of the Publisher.

First published in the United States in 1993 by
Sarpedon Publishers, Inc., New York

British Library Cataloguing in Publication Data available

ISBN 1-85367-173-8

Library of Congress Cataloging-in-Publication Data available.

Book and cover design: Libby Braden

Cover: *Black Thursday* by Art Schultz, Museum of Flight Collection, Seattle, WA
Back cover photo: Courtesy of Gerald R. Massie

10 9 8 7 6 5 4 3 2 1

MANUFACTURED IN THE UNITED STATES OF AMERICA

To the Memory of

2nd Lt. Elbert Stanley Wood
306th Bomb Group, 369th Bomb Squadron
United States Eighth Air Force
Germany: 14 October 1943

and

Pvt. Walter Raymond Wood
Battery F, 339th Field Artillery
350th Infantry, 88th Division
American Expeditionary Force
France: 27 October 1918

"Only those that are forgotten are truly dead"

Contents

MAPS

DIAGRAMS

Acknowledgments

This book, for the most part, is a traditional work of history, but it could not have been written without the testimony of eyewitnesses to the events in the air and on the ground concerning the air strike on Schweinfurt of October 14, 1943, and its aftermath. The heart of the story, narrated in Chapters 8 and 9, is therefore an oral history that depends on few written documents. It is based on innumerable telephone calls and on correspondence over a period of more than six years, reinforced with personal interviews at many of the locales mentioned in the narrative, with many persons in Europe and the United States. My gratitude for this help is extended to the following.

The story of the last mission of the *Wicked WAAC* is based on the recollections of the surviving crewmen of that aircraft: George C. Bettinger, Leland A. Dowden, Elmer W. ("Pete") Mills, and Donald E. Williams; and next of kin Mrs. Samuel F. Gerking and James R. Montana. Other members of the 306th Bomb Group to whom I am indebted include Charles T. Schoolfield, leader of the 306th on Black Thursday, and Ralph E. Ellsworth, waist gunner on the *Picadilly Commando*, a B-17 piloted by Gustave S. Holmstrom, which was lost within minutes of the *Wicked WAAC*. Russell A. Strong, historian of the 306th Bomb Group, has been unfailingly helpful, as have many members of the 306th Bomb Group Association and of the Eighth Air Force Historical Society, who

1

responded to my queries in the *8th AF News* and in *Air Force* magazine. Kenneth C. McQuitty, 95th Bomb Group; Virgil R. Moore, 305th Bomb Group; and Lyle Kenneth Vale, 388th Bomb Group, all of Columbia, Missouri, also supplied welcome advice and assistance in technical matters. Susan J. Vale enriched the text by sharing her artistic abilities in the preparation of new maps and figures.

Archivists are among the most professional and helpful individuals with whom I've ever had the pleasure to work. Among them I must single out Richard A. Boylan, Modern Military Field Branch, National Archives, and John F. Manning, Mortuary Affairs and Casualty Support Division, U.S. Army Military Personnel Center, Alexandria, Virginia. Many other personnel have provided help at the National Personnel Records Center, Military Personnel Records, St. Louis, Missouri; Office of Air Force History, Bolling AFB, Washington, DC; U.S. Air Force Historical Research Center, Maxwell AFB, Alabama; U.S. Air Force Museum, Wright-Patterson AFB, Ohio; U.S. Army Military History Institute, Carlyle, PA; and the U.S. Army Center of Military History, Washington, DC.

In England, the hospitality and assistance of Gordon, Connie, and Lloyd Richards in Oakley, Cyril J. Norman in Bedford, and Ralph Franklin in Mill Hill led me to Thurleigh and Cambridge, the American Cemetery at Madingley, and the air museum of the Imperial War Museum at Duxford. E. A. Munday at the Air Historical Branch, Royal Air Force, London, and personnel at the Imperial War Museum, London, and the Commonwealth War Graves Commission in Maidenhead produced solutions to many of the problems I encountered in researching Chapter 9, "A Funeral in Germany."

I owe a special debt to the many people in Germany who helped me reconstruct, through correspondence and interviews, the events that happened in Unterfranken on October 14, 1943, and later. First, I am grateful to M. Leichtenschlag, local editor for the Aschaffenburg *Main-Echo* in Alzenau. I'm indebted for his help in alerting the citizens of the area to my quest for information in the form of repeated newspaper articles. In Michelbach, I am especially indebted to Reinhard and Karola Kaschura, my hosts and guides for my German odyssey and interviews, and to Edgar Handlbichler, Frau Elisabeth Hofmann, Gotthard Huth, and Alfred Sticker. Wilhelm Kampfmann of Krombach and Rudi Kress of Alzenau have been particularly persistent in interviewing on my behalf witnesses to the destruction of the *Wicked WAAC* and to the parachute landing sites of its crew. They have spent many hours on my behalf. I am also grateful to Adalbert, Jürgen, and Petra Simon of Brücken; Erich Henkel of Geiselbach; Thekla Peter Weipert of Hofstädten; Otto Staab of Kälberau; Gustav Wissel, proprietor of the *Jägerklause* (hunting lodge) in Niedersteinbach; Katharina Lorenz of Omersbach; and Father Franz Ruf of Untertheres, for information and hospitality, inevitably mixed with German delicacies. Information from Luftwaffe historian Werner Girbig, and from Dr. Alois Stadtmüller, helped me round out the narrative. Dr. Stadtmüller also provided documents for my use that he collected to write his history of World War II in the Frankfurt area. I am indebted to Daniela Amann and Eleonore Loesing, formerly of Regensburg and Würtsburg, for their translations of many of these letters and documents.

Correspondents in Germany and the United States have helped with various questions about the Luftwaffe. Most of them responded to a query published, through the courtesy of Horst Amberg, in *Jägerblatt*, journal of the German Fighter Pilots Association. Luftwaffe Captain Herbert Kist, retired, of Adenauerring, a Bf-110 radio operator-navigator who participated in Second Schweinfurt, and Philipp A. Krapf of Schweinfurt were especially helpful, as was Lorenz Rasse of Livermore, California. A "thank you" to each of them. Lastly, the recollections of Eugene L. Bower and C. Robert Waterman helped flesh out the prewar character of Lieutenant Wood.

Foreword

As the bombardier on the *Wicked WAAC* on October 14, 1943, I witnessed the first half of the great air battle that has come to be known as "Black Thursday." I did not know Lieutenant Wood, the subject of this story: we met just before climbing into our B-17 that morning, and our respective duties gave us no chance to get acquainted after we did so. We parted company less than four hours later, over Germany, after a short but bitter running battle with German fighters and Destroyers. Six aircraft—an entire squadron—of our bomb group had been shot out of the air in the forty-five minutes before our B-17, too, received the damage that pulled us out of formation and onto German soil.

After arriving overseas in Bedfordshire, England, I was not in action very long. I flew one bombing mission to Gdynia, Poland, and my second half-mission as a stand-in bombardier was on Second Schweinfurt. Shot down that day, I spent much of the following year in German hospitals before my eventual repatriation and return to the United States; the events of those experiences in enemy custody are detailed in my book, *One and One Half Missions*.

Combat training in the United States covered many items, but comparing them to combat is quite another thing. Stateside training was an introduction to what "may happen," and consisted of how to strap on a parachute harness and attach the parachute, and how to don a face mask for oxygen when you felt this was necessary.

Gunnery practice was flying at a low altitude and having the gunners shoot at a stationary target.

In combat, it was necessary to forget the earlier basics and do what appeared to be the logical thing. First was to check out all operating items, for after reaching enemy territory there was little time to decide what to do. Was the oxygen working properly and was the intercom in order? The first sound of enemy Flak bouncing off the plane made one recall that in stateside training the holes made were conspicuously absent. The failure of an engine stateside meant going to a landing field for assistance, but in combat it meant sticking it out and trusting we could make it home. The loss of the main oxygen system meant going to the emergency supply, keeping in mind that the bailout bottles were to be kept aside. Our training in the field of first aid was very limited and prepared us only to deal with minor injuries (stateside we were told not to open the kit, since this would damage the contents).

On Second Schweinfurt, during a frontal attack by fighters I was struck in the leg by what later proved to be a 20mm base plate. Then the navigator, Lieutenant Wood, was shot in the stomach and I opened my first-aid kit for the first time. I used the morphine needle, placed sulpha on his wound, then packed it with cotton and bandaged it; then I prayed.

Events in the next few minutes moved quickly. Due to the loss of our second engine we could not keep up with the remaining four planes of our squadron, and this left us as sitting ducks for the German fighters. At this time someone on the plane commented that there was another bomber to the rear of us, but that was the end of that conversation and we never knew whether the plane made it. When our number-one engine caught on fire from fighters lobbing shells into us, I realized that this was the end and that we would not be returning to base; also, that we were going to go down at any time. I destroyed the bombsight with my .45-caliber automatic and threw the gun to the floor; it went down with the plane.

As I relate in my book, "The navigator, lying in back of me, touched me and pointed to his parachute and he and I put it on him and moved him to the escape hatch under the flight deck. I do not recall who pulled the release knob on the door, but I clamped his hand over the parachute release ring and pushed him headfirst out of the plane. We said something to each other at that time but I do not recall the comments we may have made. I then pulled myself back to the location of my parachute, put it on, and removed my oxygen mask and tube and placed a bailout bottle of oxygen in my leg pocket, put the end of the tube into my mouth, said another prayer and shoved myself out the door. The fact that we were flying at about 25,000 feet had no meaning."

The two interrelated books, *Or Go Down in Flame* and my *One and One Half Missions*, provide new details on the fate of those who were killed or wounded in action in the air war over Europe—details that, for the most part, are poorly documented. These are matters that many veterans do not care to discuss, even with their families, to this day. Together, however, these books will give relatives of these men deeper insight into the events of World War II that mentally and physically scarred them.

Events can become distorted when they are passed over the years from one generation to the next. But, aside from my own experience, there is enough information in the letters I received from correspondents in Germany who were witnesses to my capture to convince me that this new account of the events of "Black Thursday" is precise. Though he was not a participant in those events, author W. Raymond Wood is to be commended for a most realistic description, and for adding to our knowledge of that battle and our airmen's experience in war.

Leland A. Dowden
Stockton, California
August 1993

Introduction

Elbert S. Wood, Jr., was reported as missing in action, and later as killed in action, during the October 14, 1943, mission to destroy the ball-bearings factories at Schweinfurt, Germany. For years I was satisfied with the unembellished statement provided at the time by the Army Air Force that he had died during that operation. The telegram simply stated, with the terseness born of wartime security, that he was "killed in action on 14 October in the European area." It was not until years later that my professional work with historical materials raised my consciousness to the fact that a mass of documents exists even for modest historical events—particularly for military ones. This realization led me, in 1983, to delve into my brother's army record to see what I could recapture of his brief military career and his final combat mission.

Elbert had not only been my big brother, but also my mentor before he went away to college. Due to his example, there was no doubt in my mind I would also attend college, although I was only nine years old at the time he left home for his freshman year at the University of Missouri. He was a role model for me, yet he left home so early that I never got to know him intimately as a person. Many people retain astonishingly detailed imagery of their childhood memories: I do not, and my recollections of my brother are fleeting. Still, I recall him kneeling before me and comforting me when I was hurt as a child; drawing Bugs Bunny cartoons for me when he was home from college over Christmas; and I recall helping him with chores on our Aunt Edith's farm in Missouri, where both of us were sent every summer to keep us away from "bad influences" in a town, Gordon, Nebraska, that had little to occupy the time of young people not in school. Seeking out his military history seemed one way of getting to know both him and the times through which he lived.

Given the immensity of the American effort during World War II, tracing the fortunes of one man seemed a Herculean task. However, the activities of the common soldier during that conflict are better known than one might suspect. The endless paperwork generated by now-anonymous military clerks during World War II is, to a remarkable degree, still preserved. These records provide a paper trail that permit one to reconstruct in remarkable detail the militarily significant events in the lives of soldiers of the time.

The records of the Eighth Air Force, preserved in the National Archives, supplied the skeletal framework for the following story. The narrative was fleshed out by statements of the surviving members of his Flying Fortress aircrew, and by the testimony of German eyewitnesses to the crash of his aircraft and his funeral in the little community of Michelbach, in Bavaria, Germany. An extraordinarily detailed story eventually emerged despite the fact more than forty years had passed since the downing of his aircraft. The events of October 14, 1943, had been seared into the memories of the men shot down that day, just as the only B-17 to crash in the Michelbach area created indelible memories for witnesses on the ground in Germany.[1]

I began my quest by reading widely in Eighth Air Force literature, a selection of which is offered in the "References." This supplied a background for what the Army Air Forces had been doing in the war against Germany, but it offered nothing helpful about my brother and his aircrew. A letter to the Military Personnel Record Center in St. Louis revealed (after a wait of nearly two years!) that his service record, known as his "201 File," had been destroyed by fire in 1973.[2] This avenue of research was therefore closed.

A letter asking for information about my brother and his crew in the "Airmail" section of *Air Force* magazine brought responses from several quarters: the historian of the 306th Bomb Group, several veterans of the group, and friends of the Eighth Air Force in England. From this point on progress was rapid, although the story is impossible to tell in a strictly chronological order.

The responses to my letter directed me to the Missing Air Crew Reports (MACR) in the National Archives. One of these documents detailed the loss of my brother's B-17 Flying Fortress and the names and fate of its crew, giving also the wartime addresses of their next of kin. These letters and the information in the MACR permitted me to locate the left waist gunner, the belly turret gunner, the son of the right waist gunner, and the widow of the engineer. The latter contact led me to the bombardier. The pilot's address was later discovered in the membership list for the former inmates of Stalag Luft III. Other members of the crew were deceased and I was never able to locate their next of kin, although I was able to obtain from the Veterans Administration the dates of their death.[3]

Long and repeated telephone conversations with the four living members of the crew allowed me to reconstruct the events that took place during their mission on October 14, 1943. Visits to two of them in Arizona and California drew out further information. What was lacking, however, was information about what happened to my brother on the ground, and what happened to their Flying Fortress after it was abandoned in mid-air. The entire crew had parachuted from it after the plane was mortally damaged.

Several trips to Washington, DC were made to exploit the resources of the National Archives. Many of the original documents produced by the Eighth Air Force are preserved in their Modern Military Records repository in Suitland, Maryland. Collating my brother's "Form 5" (his flight record) with those of the missions flown by the 306th Bomb Group allowed me to narrow my search of the records to those documents relevant to my story—the documents illustrating the missions on which my brother had flown.

One unexpected by-product of my visits to Washington was

the discovery of the existence of the "293 File," or the "Individual Deceased Personnel File." Few veterans are aware of these files, for they were compiled only for servicemen who died or who remained missing in action overseas. My brother's 293 file, nearly an inch thick, contained the records of the postwar discovery of his body, his identification, and his eventual return to the United States for permanent burial. Without this record the latter half of this narrative could not have been written.

It was a moving experience to contact men in his bomb group and squadron when I attended the 1986 reunion of the 306th Bombardment Group Historical Association in Dayton, Ohio. One of the men in his squadron, Howard Sharkey, seemed to remember an Elbert S. Wood. "Let me write you when I get home," he told me. A few weeks later a thick envelope arrived from him containing two color photographs of my brother's leather A-2 flight jacket. One of the photos was of the jacket and its squadron symbol, and the other showed the jacket lining below the label, where it bore the faded but distinguishable name; "E. S. Wood." A size 38, the jacket was apparently too small for my brother, and he had turned it in, for it was reissued to Sharkey upon his arrival at the base. This discovery was of no historical importance, but it illustrates the kind of touching, intimate contacts one may make with the past at these reunions.

Another by-product of the *Air Force* magazine letter was a telephone call from the brother of another Eighth Air Force casualty who had spent many years seeking the same type of information I was after. His best advice: "Write a letter to the local German newspaper asking for information from eyewitnesses to the destruction of his bomber." The German consulate in Chicago gave me the name of the appropriate newspaper, the Aschaffenburg *Main-Echo*, and the name of the editor responsible for news in the Michelbach area. My letter to the editor asking for help resulted, several weeks later, in a short feature article in the *Main-Echo*: "*Wer erinnert sich an der Flugzeug-Abschuss 1943?*" (Who remembers the crash of an aircraft in 1943?)

For the next several weeks, letters from Germany appeared regularly in my mailbox from witnesses to the attacks on the Schweinfurt bombers and the crash of my brother's B-17. One was from the daughter of one of the soldiers who had attended his funeral. Correspondence with these people over the next two years led to a very full account of the events that took place on the ground as the Schweinfurt air battle swept over northern Bavaria and as his B-17, the *Wicked WAAC*, fell out of formation east of Frankfurt am Main. The event had left a deep impression on those who witnessed its destruction and the capture of its crew.

One of the letters supplied an unexpected piece of information. The destruction of my brother's plane and an account of his funeral in Michelbach were described in detail in a 1982 history of World War II in the Frankfurt area, written by Dr. Alois Stadtmüller, *Maingebiet und Spessart im Zweiten Weltkrieg*. The author had obtained his information from eyewitnesses to these events, and he gave them in his chapter describing the horrors of the air war over Germany. Dr. Stadtmüller later supplied me with copies of the letters and other documents he obtained from witnesses that he'd used to compile his published narrative.

In October 1988, I accepted invitations from several of my German correspondents to visit the area and see the locale where the bomber crashed, and the locations where the crewmen landed in their parachutes. I first flew to England to visit Thurleigh and my brother's former airbase near Cambridge, north of London— although the base is today off limits without special permission. I then flew to Frankfurt, rented a car, and drove east into the upper Kahlgrund region to visit Michelbach and my hosts. Over the next several days I visited the crash and parachute landing sites and photographed them, accompanied by eyewitnesses. These visits permitted me to check and cross-check the accounts by different witnesses and gain confidence in the accuracy of the story I was developing. I also photographed the sites from the air, piloted by an ex-Luftwaffe glider pilot now flying from the airport at Gelnhausen.

Standing before what had been his gravesite in the little cemetery in Michelbach, I was astonished—and disturbed, if not ashamed—to find I felt no sadness, no sense of loss, no nostalgia. On the other hand, I was numbed by the realization that my obsessive quest for information was over, and warmed by the knowledge that at last I had laid to rest the uncertainties of his combat experience and death. Elbert S. Wood, Jr., no longer remained a mere statistic, an anonymous combatant in a war that had consumed fifty million lives.

By the time I returned from Germany the story had come together in most of its detail, and I had a surer grasp of the amount and kinds of information still available for the dedicated searcher.

Many people who wish to learn more about the activities of their relatives in World War II have been frustrated by learning that the 1973 fire in the archives of the Military Personnel Record Center in St. Louis destroyed all or most of the relevant records contained there. Some 17,516,376 records were consumed in that fire, although many escaped damage. As the present account reveals, all is not lost simply because those records were destroyed, even though our subject did not keep a diary, or return home to recount his experiences. In this sense our story provides a case study of how to research a World War II military casualty. The data and addresses in the appendix are indispensable for such research on the United States Army Air Force. Readers with like interests may also find help in Dennis E. McClendon's book, *Lady be Good*, and in Susan Sheehan's *A Missing Plane*.

Following World War II, the United States Army made a monumental effort to find the graves or the remains of all U.S. military personnel who fell in battle worldwide, and to place them in military cemeteries overseas. Most Americans who lost family members during the conflict in either the European or the Pacific theaters of war had contact, in one way or another, with the American Graves Registration Command, the unit responsible for this operation. Yet it is difficult today for anyone other than a historian to discover how the remains of these men were found and identified. Just how this was done is told in Chapter 10, "The American Graves Registration Command." Many of these victims of war remain in overseas cemeteries but, at the request of their families, the remains of more than 171,000 of them were returned after the war to the United States for burial—as were those of 2nd Lieutenant Elbert S. Wood.

It is as well that forty years had passed between his death and the beginning of my search. As a teenager I was consumed by anger that he had died in a conflict I did not then comprehend. My satisfaction during the war in viewing dead and surrendering German soldiers in motion picture newsreels was perhaps understandable at the time; it would be pathological today. Four decades of reading World War II history, the healing salve of time, and the discipline forced on me by the demands of historical research have conspired to place the events of the war and his death in greater perspective, so I was able to approach the search for his story with a degree of objectivity that would have been impossible earlier.

Witnesses still too freshly scarred by wartime events sometimes find their memories prove too bitter to recall with a stranger. Indeed, one of Elbert's crew members told me that had I approached him with questions forty years ago, "I'd never have talked to you about it." On the other hand, one cannot wait much longer to interview people about events of this era, for the passage of time subtracts its witnesses at an accelerating pace.

CHAPTER ONE

A LOST AIRMAN

In the fall of 1943 the United States was locked in bitter combat with Nazi Germany and the Empire of Japan. Hitler controlled most of the European continent, and his armies had plunged deep into the Soviet Union, although they were fast losing ground and were on the defensive along most of the eastern front. Rommel and his Afrika Korps had been driven from North Africa by British and American armies, and the Allies were now poised to invade southern Europe—first Sicily, and then southern Italy. In the Pacific, the great Japanese advance had been halted and the Empire was beginning to suffer disastrous reverses: its army had evacuated Guadalcanal, its navy had lost much of its fleet in the Battle of the Bismarck Sea, and its tenuous toehold in the Aleutian Islands had been abandoned.

The tremendous industrial resources of the United States had been brought into play, not only to equip the millions of Americans newly mobilized for military service, but to buoy the fighting ability of America's allies on every front. The tide of battle was finally turning in favor of the Allies in both theaters of war, though nearly two years of savage fighting still remained. Operation OVERLORD, the invasion of France at Normandy, was still nine months distant, and its success depended largely on the Allies obtaining superiority in the air over Europe.

The United States Army's Eighth Air Force, stationed in

England, was composed of more than 200,000 men—the flesh-and-blood components of the greatest air force in history and aptly named, in postwar years, "The Mighty Eighth." The mission of that force was to destroy the foundation of the Nazi war machine by strategic bombing—the "surgical" destruction of those essential industrial elements needed to conduct modern war. Pitted against the skilled and often desperate resistance of the Germans, the Eighth Air Force lost nearly 26,000 men in the course of that long and bitter campaign. The story of their heroic efforts to carry out their often impossible orders has been told by many veterans, both by the commanders and by the men who flew the missions. Yet these stories, written by those who lived, illuminate only part of the immense human tragedy that accompanied the air war over Europe. Another part of the story can be revealed by tracing the brief but dramatic career of 2nd Lieutenant Elbert S. Wood, one of those 26,000 United States airmen who did not survive to become a veteran.

*   *   *

In October 1943, Elbert S. Wood, Sr., was the station agent for the Chicago and North Western Railroad in the little community of Cody, Nebraska. Cody was a town of 250 persons, set in the isolated Sand Hills region in the northwest part of the state. Its sand dunes, frozen in place by a mantle of prairie grasses, stretched away in every direction from the town in rolling billows of dull, brown, short grass. Wood's office in the railroad station faced south toward the hills, the view interrupted by a gray metal grain elevator and a few trees along Highway 20. Trains moving east past the station carried to market in Omaha the cattle for which the Sand Hills are famous, and other trains, moving west, often carried to Wyoming prison camps remnants of Field Marshal Erwin Rommel's Afrika Korps, captured when Tunisia fell to the Allies in May 1943.

As the station agent, Elbert Wood, Sr., served as the medium through which telegrams from the Adjutant General, by order of the Secretary of War, were delivered to the next of kin announcing casualties of war. He was to decipher, record, and personally deliver to his neighbors throughout the war many such messages announcing that a son or husband was missing or had been killed in action. Delivering these telegrams was the hardest duty he had ever had to perform. Standing in the doorway with a telegram, he could never fully conceal his emotions from a family that rarely misunderstood the reason for his hat-in-hand visit.

When the keys began tapping on the telegraph in his office on the morning of October 26, 1943, he began recording a message the arrival of which he'd always feared: one addressed to himself, Elbert S. Wood, Sr. Force of habit alone held him at his typewriter until the telegram was complete, announcing that his son, 2nd Lieutenant Elbert S. Wood, Jr., was reported missing in action since October 14 over Schweinfurt, Germany. "If further details or other information are received you will be promptly notified." It was a discouraging, but not hopeless communication, and one that left the family in helpless anticipation for two and a half months. What had happened? All that the family could do was speculate on the fact that sixty American bombers had been shot down that day—it was international news.

In late December and early January, letters and packages that had been mailed overseas to Elbert Jr. by friends and family were returned, marked "Missing in Action." False hope was given the family in a letter from a well-meaning fellow soldier who had remained in the United States as an instructor in the Army Air Force: "The boys at the field here who have been to combat say that better than 90% of the boys who went down over Germany are now working with French underground units." This improbable scenario was clearly belied by the statistics available at the time.

When the lines began transmitting his name again on January 1, 1944, the hopes of Elbert Sr. momentarily rose that the message would report that his son was a prisoner of war.

A second time he delivered a message to his family, but this one permitted only the feeble hope that the report received from the German government through the International Red Cross that his son was killed in action was, perhaps, some terrible mistake. The family was devastated.

Wood's younger brother, twelve years old, sat on a wooden fence at school for most of the day the news arrived. It was not until he was in college, a decade later, that he no longer awoke from dreams in which it was indeed all a dreadful error, and Elbert had returned from the war alive—one of the symptoms clinically known, since the end of the Vietnam War, as post-traumatic stress disorder (PTSD). Even later, look-alike strangers passed on the street or seen while shopping would be given long, if surreptitious, glances. Old emotions would momentarily resurface, illogical as they might be, before reality returned and recollections dimmed. The message "killed in action" should be final—a termination of hopes and the realization that someone is gone forever—but when death happens so far away under unknown circumstances, it is not hard to fantasize otherwise.

Other messages followed. On January 17, 1944, General Henry H. Arnold, Commanding General, United States Army Air Forces, wrote the family to express his sympathy, and a Purple Heart arrived later that month. Nothing more was received for nearly nine months. On September 25, a Summary Court-Martial was convened at the Kansas City Quartermaster Depot in Kansas City, Missouri, to dispose of the effects of Lieutenant Wood. Since the decedent had no debts, and no debtors, his father was entitled to receive all his personal effects.

Then, on September 30, 1944, the Quartermaster Depot at Kansas City wrote his parents that the United States Army Effects Bureau had received from overseas the personal effects of Lieutenant Wood. These effects consisted of his will and power of attorney, as well as his 80-pound military footlocker containing his uniforms and various belongings, including his pipes and stamp collection. They were shipped to Cody via railroad freight from Kansas City on October 6, 1944.

Two months later, on December 20, 1944, a letter was sent

from Headquarters, United States Army Air Forces, containing a list of the aircrew members who had been shot down with Lieutenant Wood, in the belief that the family might want to correspond with them. The list led Lieutenant Wood's mother to write the former crew members in the fall of 1945. She received letters shortly after from the pilot, George C. Bettinger, on September 6, 1945, and from an aerial gunner, Linden K. Voight, on September 10. They contained few details, but confirmed Wood's death.

The end of the war would bring new communications from the army. These dismal messages would concern the possible location of Lieutenant Wood's body, his identification, and queries as to the family's wishes about the disposition of his remains.

* * *

At 11:30 in the morning of March 13, 1947, Major Gustave H. Weimann, of the 466th Quartermaster Battalion (Mobile), American Graves Registration Command (AGRC), APO 171, United States Army, received a telephone call from an officer of the 15th British Missing Research and Enquiry Service (MRES),[1] stationed at Butzbach, in the state of Hessen, Germany. Great Britain maintained the Imperial (now Commonwealth) War Graves Commission for the same purpose the United States operated the American Graves Registration Command (AGRC): to recover their dead.

The RAF, however, made its own efforts to seek out its casualties. To this end the RAF's MRES established five sections, four of them for Germany and the occupied countries in Europe, and a fifth for the Far East. Its task: find and identify all RAF graves, and attempt to trace all missing RAF airmen of the Second World War. Each section had several Missing Research and Enquiry Units, which had the task of assessing the information for the 47,130 members of Bomber Command who had been killed or were presumed dead in missions to bomb Germany, as well as the thousands of other RAF personnel lost over Europe.

The RAF produced a "casualty file" much like the Missing Air Crew Report that the American air forces filed for each aircraft lost in action. Between 1944 and 1949 the RAF actively sought out crash sites and the graves of the airmen killed in them.[2] They tried to identify the individual bodies using essentially the same techniques as those used after the war by the AGRC at its Central Identification Points in Strasbourg, France, and Neuville-en-Condroz, Belgium. Isolated, individual British graves were consolidated into military cemeteries in Europe where they are today tended by the Commonwealth War Graves Commission. The British MRES and the American AGRC cooperated in their search for missing personnel and, when the MRES found American casualties, the information was transmitted to the nearest AGRC field unit.

When the MRES unit at Butzbach telephoned to notify the AGRC of its discovery of an American casualty, on March 13, 1947, the incoming message was duly recorded and filed by Major Weimann:

> American aircraft crashed 14 October 1943—at 16:00 hours—attack on Schweinfurt—1 American buried [at] Michelbach—Kreis Alzenau [map coordinates] L 51/M-96.

The grave, that of 2nd Lieutenant Elbert S. Wood, had been missed in earlier searches for American war dead in Germany.

*   *   *

Elbert Stanley Wood, Jr., was born in Gordon, Nebraska, on March 4, 1921, son of Vera Gladys Hiatt Wood and Elbert Stanley Wood. Elbert Jr. (Bert to his friends, but Elbert or Junior to his family) was an exemplary student in high school—categorized as "The Student" in his 1939 high school yearbook.

His high school buddy, Robert Waterman, remembers that "science and math seemed almost a part of him. He was intensely curious: thinking, testing, measuring, reading, talking, and understanding concepts. He'd walk into high school class with his hands full of papers ('evidence,' he called it), and with a book balanced on his left shoulder." Social and political sciences also attracted him, and classmate Eugene Bower recalls that he was concerned about the Nazi movement and its seizure of power in Germany when it was still hardly known or understood by many people, particularly high school students.

Among his social science experiments were two that illustrate his sense of humor. Robert Waterman recalls that one of Bert's observations was that "People in a society will put up with nearly anything before seeking relief or turning to authority for relief." According to Waterman, "Upon arrival at school one morning, Bert went to the men's room and hung a sign on one of the three station doors: 'Out of Order.' We checked several times during the day. The sign was still there, and students were using the two remaining toilets. Bert returned the next morning with another sign and placed it on one of the other doors. The students used the one remaining toilet until noon. At that peak load period, the custodian went to the principal to ask why the plumber was so slow fixing the toilets. Bert's social science experiment had proven its thesis and the perpetrator was never known."

One year the high school principal decided a more egalitarian approach should be used in teacher-student relations. In keeping with this policy he announced one afternoon at dismissal assembly that he would make any announcements the students had to offer. At the last moment Bert rose and hurried down the aisle to the stage and handed the principal a piece of paper. The principal, all smiles, read the note, "There will be a meeting of the Musicians Union at four o'clock in the Band Room." There was of course no Musicians Union, and no meeting. On the way home, after a long silence, Bert said, "It seemed the thing to do." Waterman recalls, "With Bert it was first things first. He enlisted and was gone before many of us realized there really was a war. It had seemed 'the thing to do.'"

After high school graduation he attended the University of Missouri and, later, the University of Nebraska as a pre-medical student. The Japanese attacked Pearl Harbor on December 7, 1941.

Enlisting in the United States Army on December 8, Bert was assigned to the Medical Corps because of his professed interest in medicine.

In early 1942, twenty-one-year-old Private Wood was giving inoculation shots to incoming inductees at a surgical hospital in Fort Knox, Kentucky. It was not an exciting army career and, longing for a more active role in the war, he volunteered for the Army Air Corps. It was an understandable choice for a young man nurtured for a decade on aerial barnstormers and on repeated viewings of the classic silent motion picture *Wings*—reinforced by heroic images of the RAF pilots who turned back the Luftwaffe in the real-life 1940 Battle of Britain.

Sent first to Victorville, California, he arrived at a classification center in Santa Ana, California, in September 1942, and went on to pre-flight school at Ellington Field, Texas. For whatever reason (his military file was destroyed by fire in 1973), his hopes of becoming a pilot were dashed there, and he was reassigned and sent to the navigation school at San Marcos, Texas. Graduating as a 2nd Lieutenant on the afternoon of June 26, 1943, he was furloughed home and then sent directly to England to serve what was to be his short tour with the Eighth Air Force as a member of the 306th Bomb Group.

He flew only five combat missions, one aborted mission, and a final mission that ended just short of the target at Schweinfurt, Germany. His Army Air Force career lasted almost exactly one year, and his active service concluded at the end of a parachute after only thirty days.

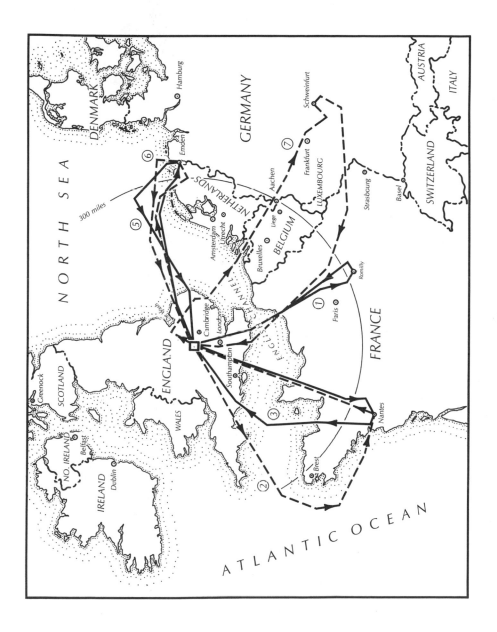

Northwest Europe, showing the combat missions flown by Lieutenant Elbert
S. Wood in September and October of 1943 (his Mission 4 is not shown: it
was recalled before reaching the coast of France). The arc shows the
300-mile radius that was the limit of fighter escorts flying from bases in East
Anglia in the fall of 1943. At this time the Eighth Air Force was only
nibbling at the margins of occupied Europe and the Third Reich.

CHAPTER TWO
AIR WAR OVER GERMANY

The air war over Germany during World War II was fought by men in machines who left few material traces of their conflict after the wreckage of downed planes had been cleaned up and recyled into new weapons of war. Today, the countryside reveals little of the conflict and only the cities of Europe retain their scars. The sky was washed clean of the fury of air combat only minutes after the action ended. Perhaps for this reason it might wrongly be thought that these air battles left little in the way of detailed history. On the contrary: most air battles resulted in great quantities of official, if impersonal, records produced both by the Allied and the German air forces. When these documents are combined with the information available from surviving aircrew members and other eyewitnesses, it is possible to reconstruct many of these battles in minute detail—more so than is possible for many naval or land engagements of comparable importance.

Air power has been overemphasized in many World War II histories—principally, perhaps, by the airmen—but there is no doubt that its overall role in defeating the Axis was a crucial one. That role was to starve the German war machine of essential resources: submarines, ball-bearings, oil, and gasoline. For this reason, as early as 1940 the Royal Air Force (RAF) Bomber Command had begun daylight bombing of Germany. The German air defenses, however, were stronger than anticipated, and that mission became

27

too hazardous to continue. RAF bombers were shot down in such large numbers that they very quickly shifted to night bombing. Bombing during the night intensified during the Battle of Britain, and accelerated again in 1942. Given the existing technology, however, trying to hit small strategic targets at night was impossible, and the practice of area bombing was developed, since large German cities were the only targets the British bombers had any chance of finding. Area bombing destroyed large areas of many German cities, obliterating industrial targets as well as (intentionally) the homes of the workers who labored in them.

The strategic directors of the United States Army Air Force (USAAF), on the other hand, considered the tactic wasteful. They believed that heavily armed aircraft using the vaunted Norden bombsight could bomb industrial targets during daylight hours with pinpoint precision and return safely to their bases. This was to be the task of the Boeing B-17 Flying Fortress and the Consolidated B-24 Liberator heavy bombers of the Eighth Air Force. The B-17 and the B-24 were large, four-engined bombers designed to carry heavy bomb loads to strategic targets deep in enemy territory. The B-17, powered by four 1,200 HP engines, had a sleek body with an art deco appearance and, by 1943, an immense vertical stabilizer that gave the plane its characteristic and unmistakable profile. A fully loaded B-17 weighed a little less than 30 tons—25 tons of plane and fuel, and a normal bomb load of three tons. It carried a crew of ten men. In the nose of the aircraft, below and in front of the pilot and co-pilot, was a cramped compartment housing the navigator and the bombardier.

Except for the pilot and co-pilot, everyone on the plane had one or more .50-caliber machine guns at his duty station. Behind the pilot and co-pilot, the ship's engineer manned the twin-gunned top turret, and the radioman aft of the bomb bay manned another gun. There was also a machine gun in each of the two waist windows back of the wing, and another two guns in the tail, manned by the tail gunner. The belly gunner, squeezed into the ball turret directly amidship, also had twin machine guns—a total of eleven guns for each Flying Fortress. Its powerful defensive armament, however, was responsible for a lessened bomb load. The B-24 was also powered by four 1,200 HP engines, and carried a crew of ten men. Its blunt nose, high wing, and twinned vertical stabilizers made it easily distinguishable from the Flying Fortress. It was capable of carrying a heavier bomb load a greater distance than the B-17, but it was a less rugged airplane and could absorb less punishment than the Flying Fortress.

Two separate American air forces were dedicated to the strategic bombing of Europe: the Eighth and Fifteenth. The Eighth Air Force, based in England, was established there in 1942 under the command of Major General Carl Spaatz, and included both bomber and fighter commands; Brigadier General Ira C. Eaker commanded Eighth Bomber Command. The Fifteenth Air Force, activated in late 1943 in Italy, was under the command of Major General James H. Doolittle. Each air force consisted of bomb groups made up of either B-17s or B-24s.

The first strategic bombing raid by the Eighth Air Force was on August 17, 1942. The target was the railroad marshalling yard at Rouen-Sotteville, in Normandy, northern France, just south of Dieppe. The twelve B-17s were led by Colonel Frank A. Armstrong, later to become the second commander of the 306th Bomb Group, and accompanied by General Eaker, commander of Eighth Bomber Command. About half the bombs struck the target, damaging tracks and destroying a few railroad cars. Some bombs also fell in the village of Rouen, causing civilian casualties—the first of many such losses, both those of occupied Europeans and, later, Germans. The bombers, however, were unscathed, save for pigeon damage to the nose cone of one of the returning aircraft.

The Combined Bomber Offensive by the British and American airmen, established by the Allied leaders at the Casablanca Conference in January 1943, became operational by June that year, and guaranteed "round the clock" bombing of the Third Reich on an almost daily basis. The RAF continued to bomb occupied Europe during the night, and the United States Eighth Air Force returned to pound other targets during the day. The goals of both were to destroy German military, economic, and industrial systems, and to undermine the morale of the German people. In the early years of the war, unescorted Allied bombers suffered staggering losses in trying to deprive Germany of these essentials. Until long-range fighters were available to escort the heavy bombers over enemy territory, the Luftwaffe exacted a terrible toll from the American bomber fleets in their raids against U-boat building yards, aircraft factories, transportation, and petroleum facilities.

Perhaps twenty-five percent of America's war production was devoted to aviation, of which more than forty percent was poured into heavy bombers—a major part of which was dedicated to strategic bombing of Nazi Europe. By the war's end, cities had been laid waste throughout Europe, but particularly in Germany. Representative statistics: thirty-three percent of Berlin; forty-three percent of Schweinfurt; fifty-two percent of Frankfurt; fifty-six percent of Emden; seventy-five percent of Hamburg; and eighty-three percent of Bonn were in ruins. More than six hundred acres in each of twenty-seven German cites were devastated, and 600,000 German civilians had been killed.[1]

On August 17, 1943, the Eighth Air Force struck two important targets, penetrating the very heart of central Germany, and reaching Schweinfurt and Regensburg. Schweinfurt was the home of important factories manufacturing ball-bearings, essential to all mechanized equipment, and Regensburg was the locale for a Messerschmitt factory. Both targets were heavily damaged during the two-pronged August 17 raid, but the cost in American men and machines was high: sixty bombers and six hundred men did not return. Although the two targets were of nearly equal importance, this mission was to become known as "First Schweinfurt."

The Schweinfurt-Regensburg mission, combined with other heavy raids on German industrial targets, convinced the Luftwaffe High Command that strong countermeasures were necessary to reduce the damage to German war production. For this reason, Destroyer (Zerstörer) units were recalled from France and from the Italian and Russian fronts to reinforce the Reich's home air defense.

The Destroyer wings (ZG, or Zerstörergeschwader) consisted of squadrons of Messerschmitt Bf-110s, twin-engined strategic fighters especially equipped for destroying the Allied heavy bombers. There were two such units: III./ZG 26 operated in the Rhineland from a base near Hannover in northern Germany, while II./ZG 76 defended central Germany from bases near and east of Frankfurt.

Because Eighth Air Force bombers flew carefully planned zigzag routes to deceive German air defenses regarding their target until the last moment, a new German tactic was evolved, called *Zahme Sau* ("Tame Boar"). As the bombers approached from England, fighters and Destroyers at airfields scattered across France and the Low Countries and in Germany were scrambled. They assembled over radio beacons that were believed to lie along the flight path of the bomber stream. The fighters attacked the bombers as long as their fuel and ammunition lasted, landed at the nearest airfield to replenish both, and assailed the bombers again. Each fighter was therefore capable of flying several sorties during the same raid, attacking the flight into Germany as well as its return home. Reichsmarshall Hermann Göring, head of the Luftwaffe, had in fact ordered pilots to fly at least two if not three such missions during each Allied raid.[2] The German intent was to break up and destroy the heavy bomber groups, if possible. Annihilating an entire group was far more devastating to the morale of bomber crewmen than the loss of a few planes in each group—and they nearly annihilated the 305th and 306th bomb groups on Second Schweinfurt on October 14, 1943.

Over time, the Combined Bomber Offensive accomplished two major ends. First, the Luftwaffe was destroyed as an effective offensive weapon, in part by destroying its planes and pilots in the air, and in part by obliterating the factories and the oil industry that produced and fueled them. Second, at least during the last sixteen months of war, the demolition of some twenty percent of

German industrial output severely curtailed Nazi war production. Incredibly, however, German production increased to its peak in mid-1944. Nevertheless, "The bottom line," as Kenneth P. Werrell concluded in his 1986 article "The Strategic Bombing of Germany," "is that the Germans had enough equipment; they lacked fuel and numbers." Lack of fuel for training resulted in a steady decrease in the quality of German replacement pilots as the conflict wore on. In the end, the greatest success of strategic bombing was denying Germany the fuel for its war machine—particularly for the Luftwaffe, giving Allied forces total control of the air in the last months of the conflict.

The aerial offensive took its toll on Nazi Germany in another way: from the first British air raids over occupied Europe until June 4, 1944, it was the equivalent, as Air Marshal Arthur ("Bomber") Harris said, of the "Second Front" demanded by the Soviets. Although Allied forces were fighting their way north after invading Italy, the Red Army was holding the bulk of the German ground forces at bay on the Eastern Front almost single-handed. The invasion of Normandy reduced the air assault on Europe to a "Third Front," but this demotion did not reduce the drain on German resources by the Combined Bomber Offensive; indeed, the raids became even more crippling. By the end of 1943, the ground defense of the Third Reich required an army of nearly two million civilian and military personnel.

Anti-aircraft defenses absorbed vast quantities of war materiel that was siphoned away and denied the German army. Thirty percent of gun production and twenty percent of the heavy ammunition was being used against hostile aircraft instead of against the Allied armies closing in on Germany from the U.S.S.R., France, and Italy. Electronic gear and optics also were diverted from front lines by the demands of radar and anti-aircraft installations. Albert Speer, writing in Spandau Prison after the war,[3] found that doubts about the American air offensive missed the decisive point. "The real importance of the air war," he wrote, "was the fact that it opened a second front long before the invasion of Europe." He concluded that, "as far as I can judge from the accounts I have read, no one has yet seen that this was the greatest lost battle on the German side."

German Flak (mercifully contracted from *Fliegerabwehrkan-none*, or anti-aircraft guns) was greatly feared by Allied fliers. Little wonder: by 1944 about 1,250,000 men and women served in this arm of the Luftwaffe—about half of its total force, not to mention the Flak units in use by the German army and navy.

Flak batteries were established at strategic locations across occupied Europe, especially around industrial targets. Large-caliber heavy Flak was capable of reaching an altitude of 35,000 feet, and depending on the caliber, a gun could fire eight to twenty rounds a minute. A crew of seven to eleven men was required in order to fire the time-fused high-explosive ammunition. Range-finders were augmented by radar sets that permitted very accurate range data to be fed to the gunners, tracking the altitude and air speed of their targets. Consequently, a few guns were capable of putting up a very respectable and very accurate pattern against incoming bombers, and heavy concentrations of them provided a very lethal barrage indeed.

Flak was feared by the bomber crews because it was totally beyond their control: one could return the fire of incoming fighters, but Flak could not be attacked; defensive flying was the only defense against this anonymous threat.

The drain in resources, as Kenneth Werrell points out, ramified throughout the Reich as new building material was requisitioned to repair damaged factories, railroads, and other installations—activities that themselves required an investment of one and a half million persons.

According to the postwar Strategic Bombing Survey, nearly 4.5 million people, or 3.6 percent of the German population, were defending their homeland against air attack and repairing its damages. The dispersal of German industrial targets proved to be effective, but this was not carried out until mid-1944, and it had its drawbacks: assembling the parts from scattered locations demanded reliable transportation. And scheduled deliveries became a thing of the past when the Luftwaffe could not restrain the free-ranging P-51 Mustang, P-47 Thunderbolt, and P-38 Lightning fighters from their forays over Germany, and when safe passage for any vehicle—on either highways or rail lines—was in jeopardy. Little wonder that "death by fighter-bomber" (*Jäbotod*) became a stock phrase for those who lost their lives traveling on German roads or railroads.

Critics of strategic bombing have noted that German production rose markedly throughout the bombing campaign—thanks largely to the efforts of Albert Speer, the German armaments minister—and, contrary to all Allied expectations, achieved its peak when the air offensive also was at its greatest. "The important consequence of the bombing," according to R. J. Overy, "was not that it failed to stem the increase in arms production, but that it prevented the increase from being very considerably greater than it was."[4]

By the summer of 1944 the Luftwaffe had been whittled down to a small force that was increasingly powerless against the Allied air armadas over Europe. Allied long-range fighter escorts kept enemy fighters away from the bombers and protected their formations from being broken up as they had been during First and Second Schweinfurt.

There is no question that air power and strategic bombing were vital elements in the destruction of the Third Reich. Indeed, despite extensive preparations for anti-aircraft defense, air superiority permitted some Allied troops to go ashore at Normandy and witness only two hostile aircraft over the beaches.

The Luftwaffe flew barely 300 sorties on invasion day, in contrast to more than 10,000 by the Allies. Such air superiority could not have been gained without the elimination of the Luftwaffe through the reduction of its machinery by bombing its factories, and by smashing the sources of its fuel supply. It was undoubtedly fuel that was the more decisive, however, for by mid-1944 the Luftwaffe lacked the fuel to fly more than a fraction of its available arsenal. The Allied oil offensive had found the Achilles heel of its adversaries. World War II would have lasted much longer, and would have been far more costly in men and equipment—for both sides—had the Allied air offensive not been successful.

CHAPTER THREE

PROSPECTS FOR SURVIVAL

The 306th Bomb Group was one of the first such units to become operational in the Eighth Air Force in Great Britain, having been the fifth such group to go overseas. The ground echelon of the 306th, together with that of the 93rd Bomb Group, made its way across the Atlantic in 1942 crowded onto the world's largest ship, the HMS *Queen Elizabeth*. The nearly 500 ground-service personnel of the 306th were only a small part of the approximately 15,000 men wedged aboard the ship. It took only four days to make the trip despite the extra time consumed by the ship's constant zigzagging, a precaution against German submarines patrolling the North Atlantic.

The men disembarked in Scotland at Greenock on the Firth of Clyde—near Glasgow—on September 5, and boarded a train for an all-night ride to their base. They detrained at a station near the small town of Thurleigh, and were taken by truck for a short ride to the nearby base. The air echelon arrived the following week.

Thurleigh is in Bedfordshire, sixty airline miles northwest of the heart of central London, and five miles north of Bedford. Bedfordshire, or "Beds," is a small county in East Anglia, drained by the river Great Ouse. The country is low and rolling, much of it lying only a few feet above sea level.

East Anglia has the richest agricultural land in Britain, and merits the nickname "the granary of England." The Ouse has cut

37

a broad valley through its gently rolling hills, and the river follows a meandering path to the northeast that carries its waters past Bedford, the county seat of "Beds," then into the broad bay known as The Wash, and at last into the North Sea.

Thurleigh is a small rural community that consisted then, as now, of a few hundred people, set on the slopes of low, rounded hills. The road to town passes the ruins of an ancient stone wind-mill, then the post office and the white-washed "Jackal" pub, and several of the thatched cottages that characterize the countryside and that still make parts of Thurleigh resemble a scenic picture postcard. The road curved out of town and across rolling hills to the level upland beyond, and to the guardhouse at the base perimeter. This was the "Old England" of thatched cottages and Roman ruins—one of which lay just south of the runways at the home of the 306th Bomb Group. When the wind was from the southeast, the B-17s flew directly over the village as the men and planes went to work, their motors shaking the homes of its residents to their foundations.

The airbase at Thurleigh, Station No. 111, lay on an immense, level plain two miles northwest of town. It was built in the early 1940s for the RAF, and in 1942 and 1943 it was enlarged to provide accommodations for American heavy bombers. By the latter part of 1943 the base had fifty hardstands on which the Fortresses were dispersed around the perimeter track that enclosed the three main runways. Before the arrival of the 306th Bomb Group, Thurleigh had been home to an RAF Operational Training Unit and a base for Wellington bombers, but the airdrome was later occupied by a Polish RAF bomber unit. The Poles began a custom the men of the 306th continued: they inscribed in candle smoke on a mess hall ceiling the names of the cities they had bombed on the Continent.

On December 9, 1942, Thurleigh was formally transferred from the RAF to the USAAF, the first such transfer of a base in Great Britain.[1] Colonel Charles B. Overacker received the station from Squadron Leader D. A. Batwell. It was to be the home of the 306th until the end of the war, and it returned to British control on December 8, 1945.

The 306th Bomb Group consisted of four squadrons of six aircraft each: the 367th, the "Clay Pigeons"; the 368th, the "Eager Beavers"; the 369th, the "Fightin' Bitin' "; and the 423rd, the "Grim Reapers." The 414th ASG (Air Support Group) also was assigned to the base. Thurleigh was also headquarters for the 40th Bomb Wing. This wing consisted of the 92nd, 305th, and 306th bomb groups. An Air Division consisted of three such wings of three bomb groups, and in the fall of 1943 the First Air Division was composed of the First, Fortieth, and Forty-first Combat Wings.

The 306th became operational with its first practice wing formation flight to The Wash on September 28, 1942. The target of its first mission was the great Compagnic de Fives Lille, a steelworks and locomotive and freight car factory at Lille, France. The Luftwaffe was more aggressive that day than on any previous raid, and the Lille mission developed into the first great aerial battle fought by the Eighth Air Force.

The first attack on German soil, however, did not take place until January 27, 1943, with a raid on Wilhelmshaven. The mission was led by Colonel Frank Armstrong of the 306th, the oldest operational group in the command. This fact led to the proud claim that the 306th, of the American bomb groups in England, was "First Over Germany."[2] The most famous novel about the air war over Europe, *Twelve O'Clock High*, was written by Captain Bierne Lay, once a 306th Bomb Group administrative and combat officer, who flew, among other missions, on the August 17 Schweinfurt-Regensburg mission. Captain Lay served, as did his co-author, Major Sy Bartlett, on the staff of General Ira C. Eaker at Eighth Air Force Command Headquarters—code-named "Pinetree"—at High Wycomb, west of London.

In the early months of 1943 the 369th Squadron, the "Fightin' Bitin'," established the enviable record of completing forty-two consecutive missions without the loss of a plane.[3] This near-miraculous record began with the first attack on Wilhelmshaven, but their run of good luck abruptly ended on July 29, 1943, during an attack on Kiel, when they lost four bombers. The record they set for consecutive no-loss missions remained intact until after the Allied landings in Normandy, however, a fact all the more impressive when one considers that during this period opposition from the Luftwaffe was at its fiercest.

The end of the luck of the "Fightin' Bitin'" squadron in July 1943 heralded bad news for most other Eighth Air Force groups as well, for losses began to mount sharply. The bloody summer of 1943 saw tremendous losses by the Eighth on its first unescorted strikes into Germany. The Schweinfurt-Regensburg mission of August 17 cut so deeply into the aircraft and manpower of the Eighth that it took nearly a month to build the force back to the point where it could mount another large raid. This mission was to Stuttgart on September 6. The losses were again very high, and for the next several weeks missions were restricted to targets in the occupied countries that could be protected by a fighter umbrella.

The prospects were dismal for an airman to survive the horrendous losses being suffered at the hands of the Luftwaffe at this time. Colonel Budd J. Peaslee (who was to be the air commander for Second Schweinfurt) has stated that "in the months preceding the second mission to Schweinfurt, the future of an individual in the combat crew of a heavy bomber was a prognostic equivalent of a victim of deep-seated cancer."[4] Every group, of course, had its own statistics based on its own losses. The 306th, for instance, lost not a single aircraft on First Schweinfurt, but was to lose ten of its fifteen Fortresses that penetrated German airspace on Second Schweinfurt.

The 120-percent loss of heavy bombers by the Eighth Air Force in the preceding four months was telling. Simple arithmetic by anyone concerned yielded a ten-percent loss per mission, so with the twenty-five-mission limit of the time, the last fifteen missions would be flown on borrowed time. It was a rare crew that earned the coveted training assignments back in the United States after completing their twenty-five missions, as the 91st Bomb Group's

Above: Elbert S. Wood, Sr., in Cody Nebraska, 1945.

Right, top to bottom: Soon-to-be B-17 navigator Elbert S. Wood, Jr., before the war. On the farm in Missouri, 1936; at the University of Nebraska; with a friend at a 4th of July picnic, 1941.

LAST WILL AND TESTAMENT

I, *ELBERT S. WOOD, JR*, a legal resident of *CODY*
(Name of testator)   (City, town, or
*CHERRY*_____, *NEBRASKA*_____United
county)   (State or district)
States of America, now in the active military service as a *2d LIEUTENANT*,
(Grade)
Army Serial Number *O-683365*, in the Army of the United States, being of sound
and disposing mind, memory, and understanding, do hereby make, publish, and declare
this instrument as my last WILL and TESTAMENT, in manner following, that is to say:

1. I hereby cancel, annul, and revoke all wills and codicils by me at any time
heretofore made;

2. I hereby give, devise, and bequeath to *MRS VERA M. WOOD*
(Name of person or persons who are
_____*MOTHER*_____, now residing in *CODY*
to inherit, with relationship, if any)   (City, town, or
*CHERRY*_____, *NEBRASKA*_____, *UNITED STATES*
county)   (State or district)   (Country)
all of my estate and all of the property of which I may die seized and possessed,
and to which I may be entitled at the time of my decease, of whatsoever kind and
nature, and wheresoever it may be situated, be it real, personal, or mixed, abso-
lutely and forever;

3. I hereby nominate, constitute, and appoint *ELBERT S. WOOD, SR.*
(Name of executor or executrix
_____*FATHER*_____, of *CODY*_____, *CHERRY*,
with relationship if any)   (City, town, or county)
_____*NEBRASKA*_____, United States of America, as my executor
(State or district)
(executrix) and request that he (she) be permitted to serve without official bond or
without surety thereon, except as required by law;

4. I hereby authorize and empower my executor (executrix) in his (her) absolute
discretion to sell, exchange, convey, transfer, assign, mortgage, pledge, invest,
or reinvest the whole or any part of my real or personal estate.

5. It is my will that no other action shall be had in the county court in the
administration of my estate than to prove and record this will and to return an
inventory and appraisement of my estate and list of claims.

IN WITNESS WHEREOF, I have hereunto set my hand and seal to this my last WILL and
TESTAMENT, at *AAFNS, SAN MARCOS, TEXAS*_____, this *JUNE 25*
(Place of execution)
day of 194*3*.

Elbert S. Wood Jr (SEAL)
(Signature of testator)

Signed, sealed, published, and declared by the above-named testator, *ELBERT*
(Name of
*S. WOOD, JR.*_____, to be his last WILL and TESTAMENT in the
testator)
presence of all of us at one time, and at the same time we, at his request and in his
presence and in the presence of each other, have hereunto subscribed our names as
witnesses, and do hereby attest to the sound and disposing mind of said testator and
to the performance of the aforesaid acts of execution at *AAFNS*_____
(Place of execution)
SAN MARCOS, TEXAS, this *25* day of *JUNE*_____, 194*3*

Howard W. Gordon   *Brooklyn, N.Y.*
John David McAllister   *St. Louis Missouri*
J.J. Kilmurick   *Phila., Pa.*

Lieutenant Wood's last will and testament. It was made on June 25, 1943,
the day after he was certified, and the day before graduation ceremonies
were held at the San Marcos, Texas, navigation school.

Lieutenant Elbert S. Wood in Central Park, New York City, July 1943.

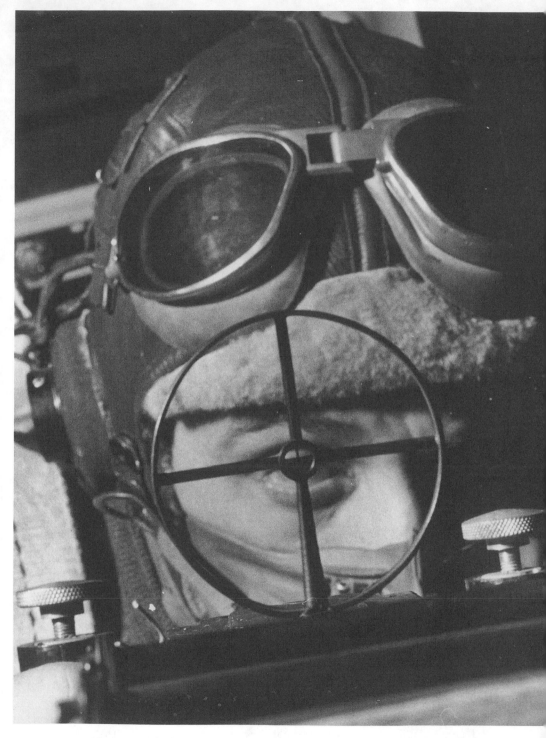

Above: A waist gunner taking aim. (Courtesy of Mrs. Gerald R. Massie)

Facing page: A pilot pushing his parachute through the escape hatch of a Fortress. (Courtesy of Mrs. Gerald R. Massie)

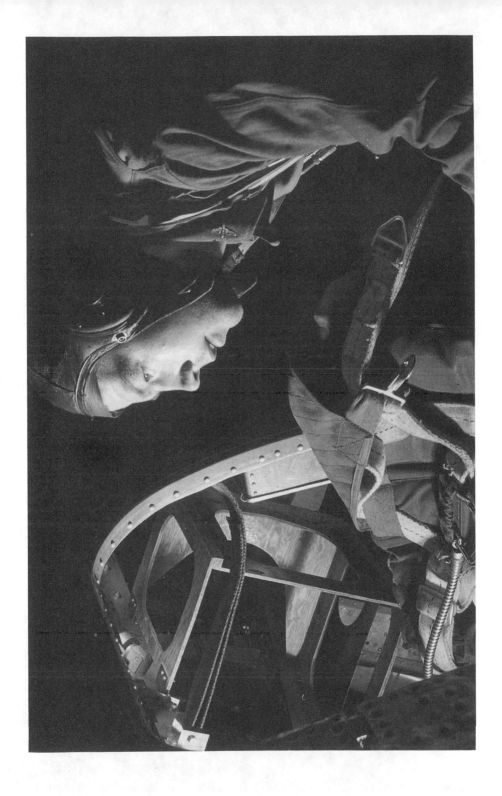

The arrival of the USAAF in England meant the beginning of round-the-clock bombing by Allied forces. (Courtesy of Squadron/Signal Publications)

Two postcards from pre-flight school, and a V-Mail letter from England: "Made it safe and sound."

Aerial view of Thurleigh, Station 111, taken August 6, 1945. Individual B-17s are visible on their hardstands. The four bomb squadrons were positioned as shown around the perimeter track; the bomb dump (BD) was in the wooded area in the upper left of the photograph. (Crown copyright. Property of the British Air Ministry, courtesy of Ralph Franklin.)

Above: A thatched cottage along the main road in Thurleigh, Bedfordshire.
Below: A B-17 squadron over the English Channel.
(Courtesy of Gerald R. Massie)

Noteworthy achievements and other tasks of the "American Nose Art Command." (Courtesy of Squadron/Signal Publications)

Facing page: The First Combat Wing, First Air Division, en route through partial cloud cover to a target in Europe. (Courtesy of Gerald R. Massie)

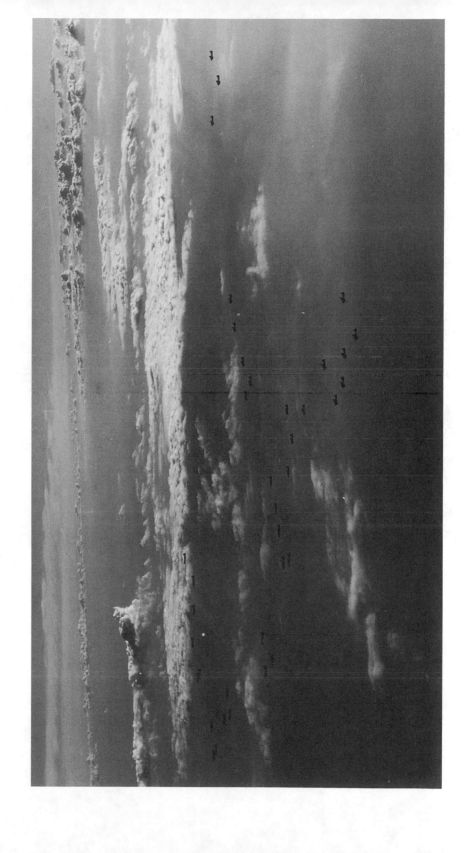

Flying Fortresses of the 381st Bomb Group, 533rd and 534th squadrons, in line awaiting takeoff at Ridgewell, England. (Smithsonian Institution Photo No. 65330)

Above: A city that purchased enough war bonds could be rewarded with their "own" Flying Fortress.
Below: Other B-17s were more expediently (or optimistically) named.
(Courtesy of Squadron/Signal Publications)

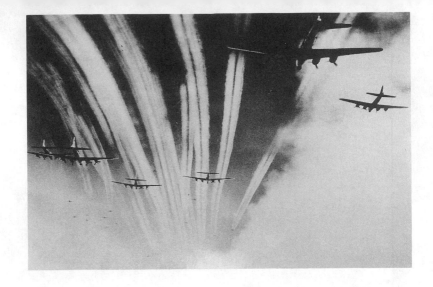

The journey into the "wild blue yonder" could sometimes have a harrowing conclusion. (Courtesy of Squadron/Signal Publications)

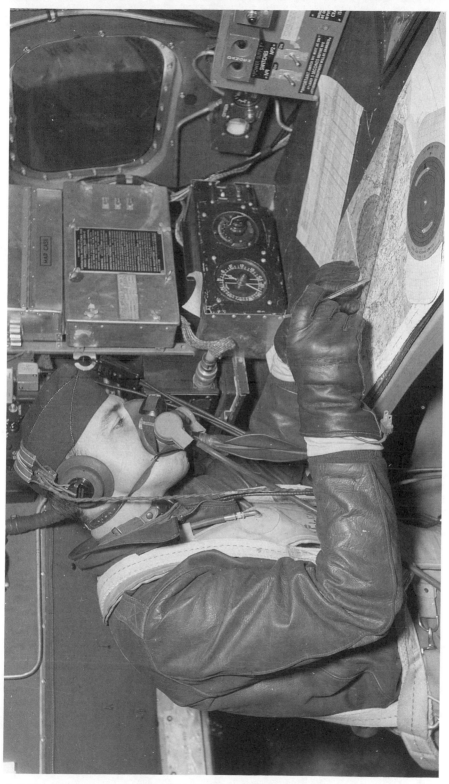

A B-17 navigator at his worktable. (Smithsonian Institution Photo No. 69381)

Front view of a bomb group. The contrails became more pronounced as
altitude was gained. (Courtesy of Gerald R. Massie)

Fortress *Memphis Belle* did in June 1943. When conditions became less severe in March of the following year, the tour of duty was extended to thirty missions.

*   *   *

That part of the Luftwaffe assigned to defend the Third Reich was at the peak of its prowess in the fall of 1943. Fighters had been drawn in from Hitler's far-flung fronts to defend the homeland from the disaster raining down, day and night, on its cities. There was as yet no intimation that Germany was about to lose control of the skies: fighter strength would, indeed, never be greater, and within a year the miraculous jet fighters under development would be deployed against the enemy air armadas overhead.

The German air force had risen in secret from the ashes of the first World War. The Versailles Treaty had prohibited military aviation, but the postwar German Reichswehr skirted this prohibition, sometimes in the most unexpected fashion. An agreement with the Soviet Union provided a secret training station for its fliers in Russia—an agreement that kept these activities beyond the sight of League of Nations observers. Beginning in 1926, long before the Nazis took power, Reichswehr personnel were being sent to Lipetsk, an airfield 220 miles southeast of Moscow and more than a thousand miles east of Berlin. Leading pilots of what would become the Luftwaffe trained there, in many cases flying prototypes of combat planes that would be used in the coming conflict.[5]

The creation of the Luftwaffe itself began in 1933, shortly after Hitler was named chancellor of Germany. Lipetsk was closed down, and covert installations were built in Germany itself. Hitler made Hermann Göring, a World War I fighter ace of the Richthofen Geschwader, responsible for creating the new air force. Göring had been an excellent fighter pilot, and in the early years he succeeded in creating a first-class fighting force. The reason: he inherited well-designed warplanes from the Reichswehr (masquerading as civilian aircraft), augmented by the hard work of astutely chosen and talented associates. But being a fine pilot does not mean one is also a brilliant, or even an adequate, strategist. As the war went on, Göring's intellectual and personal failings meant that the Luftwaffe performed well in spite of its founder and leader.

The existence of the Luftwaffe as an independent military unit was openly announced in March 1935, when Hitler felt Germany was strong enough to defy the Versailles Treaty. The Luftwaffe now consisted of 1,888 planes and 20,000 officers and men. By 1936, new aircraft—unexcelled in quality by any other air force in the world—were being produced. Some of them were tested—as were tactics later to be used in blitzkrieg—during the Spanish Civil War.[6]

The strength of German air power became fully apparent in the September 1939 blitzkrieg in Poland, when the Luftwaffe and the Wehrmacht worked in tandem to establish the pattern that would be so successful in future campaigns. The Luftwaffe now possessed 3,560 combat aircraft. Brought to bear on any one front, and for a limited duration, they could affect the outcome of a campaign.[7]

The Luftwaffe continued to grow after the Polish campaign, and by 1940 it boasted 4,000 combat aircraft. The tactics this force employed in the blitzkrieg in France in 1940, and in Russia in 1941, were brilliant. But the fact that German aircrews were shortly being scattered between fronts in Russia, Scandinavia, North Africa, on the Atlantic coast, and over Germany itself meant that the impact of this powerful "mailed fist" had become dissipated.

The Luftwaffe was doomed to lose the 1940 Battle of Britain from the start, although its outcome was, for a time, bitterly contested. The vulnerability of the German bombers to fighter attack; the lack of a large four-engined bomber (halted in favor of dive bombers) capable of carrying heavy bomb loads; and the vascillating targets Göring chose for attack meant that they never concentrated on one objective long enough to have a decisive effect. The English were able to maintain a steady supply of fighter planes for the battle—although finding pilots for them was a major bottleneck. On the other hand, the Germans lost irreplaceable, highly trained aircrews in this futile campaign—losses that would affect future campaigns. In the final analysis, although the Luftwaffe was the most formidable air force in the world at the start of the battle, the assignment given it by Hitler to annihilate the fighter element of the strong and skillful RAF, over English ground, proved far beyond the ability of the Germans at the time.

The disastrous loss of British bombers over Heligoland Bight during the "Phony War" in December 1939 revealed a truth that had to be learned anew with every strategic bombing campaign: unescorted bombers were at the mercy of enemy fighters.[8] German losses were prohibitive in the Battle of Britain—so they shifted to night attacks. English losses were devastating when they bombed Germany during the day—so they shifted to night attacks. American losses in daylight attacks over Germany also were prohibitive— until long-range fighter escorts became available.

The Eighth Air Force began its buildup in England for the aerial destruction of Germany in 1942. By July 1943, fifteen groups of B-17s and B-24s were operational. At this time the P-47 Thunderbolt fighters were able to escort bombers only to the coasts of Holland and Belgium, but in July auxiliary wing tanks were introduced that permitted them to accompany bombers to the German border. In this manner they could return to base, refuel, and meet their "big friends" again on their way home.

The number of day fighters for the defense of German soil rose slowly to counter the growing destruction of German industry. From 120 aircraft in March 1943, the total rose to its all-time high at the end of August, when 405 Messerschmitt Bf-109s and Focke-Wulf 190s were augmented by nearly a hundred twin-engined Messerschmitt 110s and 410s. Many of the aircraft had been pulled back from active fronts—from Italy, France, and Russia—to defend the homeland. The effect on front-line actions is easy to surmise, but the result was also the decimation of the American bombers. In July, even before its peak strength was achieved, the Luftwaffe shot down ten percent of the attacking American air fleets.

Early 1944 was to see the accelerated decline of the Luftwaffe, but for the American bombers in the bloody summer of 1943 this eclipse was not yet predictable. The arrival of the P-51 long-range escorts for the bombers was the first element that would turn the air war around. During "Big Week" (February 20–25), seventy-five percent of the German aircraft industry was damaged. In the first four months of 1944, 1,000 German day pilots were lost in combat, many of them from training schools. The use—and loss—of pilots and other trained personnel from Luftwaffe training schools was to have serious consequences on the production of pilots. The Russian front, and Stalingrad in particular, had bled the Luftwaffe dry on the eastern front, and now a fatally weakened Luftwaffe was fighting for its very survival. These events, however, lay in the future, and for the time being the Americans had to learn that the Luftwaffe was capable of inflicting near-mortal damage on their unescorted bombers.

CHAPTER FOUR

INTO THE ARENA

Elbert S. Wood was among the members of the first graduating class of the United States Army Air Force Navigation School at San Marcos Air Field, Texas, on June 26, 1943. Wood arrived there from Pre-flight School at Ellington Field, Texas, for an intensive, twenty-week course in which he spent 782 hours in ground-school classes and 104 hours in the air in practical navigation training in Beechcraft and Lockheed "Navigators." It was rigorous training and, in April, he wrote his sister Marjorie that "School is about half over now, and is getting a little easier. From now on there will be more flying and less classroom work. These fourteen-hour school days are beginning to get pretty old!" Little wonder: reveille was at 5:45 a.m., classes were from 7 a.m. to 9 p.m., lights out at 9:30 p.m., and a bed check at 9:35 p.m.

The ground school included instruction in pilotage, instruments, dead reckoning, radio, celestial navigation, meteorology, and code and recognition. After completing the course, graduates were awarded navigator's wings, commissioned second lieutenants, and furloughed home before being sent to their units for further training. Different assignments called for different instruction, and the Eighth Air Force supplied indoctrination and procedural training for its men at its duty posts.

The 353 newly minted lieutenants of the graduating class were sent to duty stations throughout the world, most of them to navigate

Flying Fortress or Liberator bombers. Eleven of them went to the
306th Bomb Group in England as part of the buildup of the Eighth
Air Force in SICKLE, the code for the bomber offensive against
Germany. It was, unfortunately, not a propitious time to become
a member of the Eighth Air Force. Seven of these eleven young
navigators were to die in combat (three of them on Second
Schweinfurt) or in air accidents in Europe, and two others were shot
down to become prisoners of war in the five-month period
beginning in October 1943. Only two men completed their tour of
duty. Such were the odds of surviving air combat in the fall and
winter of 1943–44.

On his furlough, in July, Lieutenant Wood visited his family
in Nebraska, where he asked his mother for another photograph.
The photo of his forty-two-year-old, but youthful-looking, mother
had been stolen by a fellow soldier, presumably to grace a locker
or wallet lacking in feminine charms. After this brief visit home,
and bidding what was to be a final farewell to his family, his orders
carried him to Fort Slocum, New York. He was able to visit his sister
Marjorie in New York City before departure. There he took in some
of the sights, including Central Park. Whatever rumors he'd
received of his future duty made him fatalistic about his chances
of survival, for he grimly told her, "I won't be coming back." By
August 2 he was in England, and a few days later wrote home,
"Made it safe and sound. I am located in a pretty part of England,
but things are not as convenient here. We have to walk to town if
we want to go in. The people are very friendly and talkative, and
very curious about the U.S.A. The quarters are good here, and the
food, too."

Air Transport Command flew the planes overseas and the
bomber crewmen usually were passengers. They flew the Atlantic
Ocean on what was known as the "Atlantic Bridge"—from Gander
Lake, Newfoundland, overnight—and landed in Scotland. Ralph
Ellsworth, a 369th gunner, said, "They threw our parachutes into
the bomb bay, and told us that we wouldn't need them, because
we'd freeze in the water in a few minutes, anyway, if we went down.

I was in the nose, and when the heater quit working, big balls of frost formed on the windows. The pilot made me stay there to maintain aircraft trim; he didn't want to work any more than he had to. When the de-icer quit working we came down and flew just over the waves to get the ice off the wings."

Crews arriving in England went first to a Combat Crew Replacement Center (CCRC), sometimes described as a "finishing school for combat." Lieutenant Wood went directly to the 11th CCRC at Bovingdon, an air base ten miles northwest of London. Like all new crewmen, he would not go into combat for several weeks. Despite his training, a great deal remained to be learned above and beyond the basics already learned at navigation school. There was a second such center in England, at Cheddington, established to indoctrinate arriving heavy-bomber crews in the problems and procedures of air war in the European theater of war and, equally important, to complete their specialized training. These were large establishments, consisting of an airfield with associated buildings for classrooms and artificial trainers. The center had three separate schools: one for B-17 crews, another for B-24 crewmen, and a third for gunners only.

The new crews assembled in lecture halls to receive instruction for two days of eight hours or more. Lectures covered a multitude of related topics, including the history and development of the Luftwaffe, as well as its strategy, tactics, and its planes and equipment; the recognition of enemy and friendly aircraft through charts and models; analyses of targets recently struck by the Eighth Air Force and the RAF; instruction in the British Air-Sea Rescue system; and information on how to conduct oneself if taken prisoner or, under happier circumstances, techniques of escape and evasion. The information given was intensely practical. Every crew member, for example, had to know how to properly use the A-12 oxygen mask, and the necessity for shaving before a mission. A beard stubble not only was uncomfortable because the mask chafed the skin and made one itch from the constant friction during flight, but leakage could reduce one's oxygen supply as much as five percent.

There were also drills on the use of the British chest parachute, standard issue in the European theater, and ditching and dinghy drill. After the first two days, the crews were split up. Gunners were sent on to special CCRC gunnery schools, but other crew members remained for more specialized training. The intricacies of combat and survival obviously could not be learned in only two days, and the men continued to receive instruction later after reporting to their operational bases.

Navigators and radio operators were given especially rigorous instruction. Lieutenant Wood made several local training flights, in addition to simulated flights in trainers. Most flights were local, to neighboring fields at Little Staughton, Grafton Underwood, Bovingdon, and Burtonwood in the English Midlands. Techniques of navigating by dead reckoning were also reviewed until each man was proficient. Each navigator was to have an operational test when his specialized training began. Wood's operational training in B-17s began on August 12 and continued intermittently until August 23. His five flights, a total of twelve and a half hours in the air, were made with a Lieutenant Hogan and a Captain Richie.

On most combat missions the lead navigator had the responsibility of finding the target, but other navigators also had to know their position in the event the lead navigator aborted or was shot down. Navigators kept the other crew members informed of their position so they knew when to expect enemy fighters, Flak, and the arrival of their own fighter cover. The navigator also had to know their position if they were disabled and had to return to base on their own, or plot a course for, say, Sweden or Switzerland if they were too badly damaged to return home.

*   *   *

His early training at Bovingdon finished, Lieutenant Wood was given a weekend leave, which he spent in London, sightseeing and becoming acquainted with the American Red Cross Officers Club. He went on to Thurleigh on Sunday evening, August 29, and was assigned to the crew of Lieutenant George C. Bettinger, who had only recently moved from being a co-pilot to first pilot. Bettinger's newly assigned crew needed training, so they flew locally in East Anglia for the first two weeks of September. During these training flights, navigators tried to commit to memory the geography of East Anglia, both from the air and from their charts. The tightly spaced small towns looked a great deal alike until repeated visits permitted them to distinguish one hamlet from another. Instant recognition was a necessity in the event they returned badly shot up, for East Anglia was dotted with dozens of Eighth Air Force bases. Crews nevertheless often landed at the wrong field. Group commanders scheduled training flights on days when missions over Europe were impossible because of weather conditions. Crews trained in the United States had learned their trade in the arid Southwest, where flying conditions were generally ideal—and where errors elicited criticism but did not lead to the loss of aircraft.

On August 19, Lieutenant Wood was again sightseeing in London. Catching a train at Milton Ernest for a mid-week leave, his train moved south across the English lowlands, through Bedford, Flitwick, Luton, and Frogmore, and pulled into St. Pancras Station in north London about an hour later. Most arriving servicemen took a cab from the station to the downtown area. Like thousands of other servicemen on leave, he visited Buckingham Palace, Whitehall, the Houses of Parliament and Big Ben, London Bridge, "and the part that was bombed, too, and burned out," Wood wrote home to his family. A visit to London took one away from the base but, in a sense, it brought fliers closer to the war, seeing first-hand the effects the German air raids were having on the city. Bomb-damaged streets were roped off, but the cratered streets and shattered, charred buildings were visible to everyone. Airmen were usually given a seventy-two-hour pass, enabling them to stay overnight in the city before returning to their base. On August 28 he was freed to take another sightseeing tour of London, this time visiting Westminster Abbey—"a really impressive place," said Elbert.

On September 8 came good news. "Extras" appeared on the streets in the United States, and even more joy among members of the armed forces—the news of Italy's surrender to the Allies was made public. Five days earlier, troops of the British Eighth Army, under the direction of General Sir Harold Alexander, invaded the southern tip of Italy from Sicily in operation BAYTOWN and established the first Allied bridgehead on the continent of Europe. The weaker member of the fascist Axis collapsed at this threat, and gave, for the fliers who almost daily faced death in the air, a much needed lift in morale. The next day, the United States Fifth Army, under the direction of Lt. General Mark W. Clark, also invaded Italy near Salerno and after a fierce battle established a firm second beachhead. Although the Italian government quickly surrendered, the Germans reinforced their troops in Italy to resume its defense, and the Allied climb up the peninsula was to be bitterly contested.

There was other news—bad news—which the Eighth Air Force was to learn in the air, not over the radio or in the *Stars and Stripes*: "By the end of August, under pressure of the American daylight offensive, the [German] home defense force reached its all-time 'high' in first-line aircraft: 405 Me 109s and Fw 190s, plus one twin-engined Geschwader with about eighty Me 110s and Me 410s."[1]

*　　*　　*

Romilly-sur-Seine, sixty-five airline miles upriver from Paris, was a popular target for the Eighth Air Force. Beginning in December 1942, it was struck repeatedly, for Romilly was the home of a major Luftwaffe repair unit and the servicing base for Luftflotte 3, the German air fleet for all of France and the Low Countries. In addition, several aircraft plants were there, including reserve aircraft for Luftflotte 3 bases. Its location on the river made Romilly easy to find, and the opportunity to destroy fighter aircraft on the ground made it a tempting target for the Allies. Mission 95 of the Eighth Air Force on September 15 was designed to accomplish this end.

The raid on Romilly was Lieutenant Wood's first combat mission, but was mission 95 for the USAAF in England. Because the target posed no difficulties for a novice navigator, he was assigned to fly with an experienced pilot, Lieutenant Immanuel J. ("Manny") Klette. This was the first mission Klette had flown since his twenty-fifth on August 24. Returning from Villacoublay, France, with two engines lost to Flak, he lost a third engine in the traffic pattern over Thurleigh and just barely landed his B-17 on one flat tire with one engine remaining.

Klette's B-17 Flying Fortress was an F model, Serial No. 42-30199. Flying Fortresses were built not only by their parent corporation, the Boeing Airplane Company, but some were made under contract by the Douglas and Vega companies. Serial No. 42-30199 specifies that she was built in the Seattle, Washington, plant by Boeing as the sixty-eighth airplane of the one hundred B-17s of Batch 90, ordered in 1942 under Army Air Force Order No. ac-20292. She was the 30,199th airplane ordered from the aircraft industry in 1942, and was the 2,114th B-17 of the 12,761 built during World War II. The plane, produced at a cost of $316,426, rolled off the assembly line in April 1943, and was accepted into the USAAF inventory by an Air Force representative on April 22. The additional cost to equip and train the air and ground crew for a heavy bomber was about $100,000, bringing the total cost for such a combat unit to nearly half a million dollars—at a time when a dollar an hour was a good wage.

The aircraft record card for 42-30199 notes that she was then flown to the Cheyenne Modification Center, in southeastern Wyoming, on April 26. There, the Fortress was modified for the weather and combat conditions expected at her final and as yet still secret destination: England. After several other stops and checkout flights, she left the United States in August 1943 for assignment with the Eighth Air Force under shipping code UGLY/SOXO, a designation for materiel sent to that part of the United Kingdom north of London.

Sometime after its arrival in England, the plane was informally christened the *Wicked WAAC* (referring irreverently to the Women's Army Auxiliary Corps), and a woman's figure, clad in briefs, astride a falling bomb, was painted on the left side of the nose of the plane. The Fortress was painted olive drab on its upper surfaces, and a neutral grey on its underside. It carried the squadron designation (WW) on the fuselage sides, and the letter R on its tail below the serial number. There are no known photographs of the plane.

Klette was scheduled to fly the fourth position, behind Captain Charles T. Schoolfield's plane, which led the lead group. Flying with the 369th Squadron and Captain Schoolfield and Lieutenant Klette were Lieutenants B. C. Bryant, W. H. Lockyear, R. W. Porter, G. F. Thomas, and their crews.

Second Lieutenant Abraham Block was the co-pilot on the mission; 1st Lieutenant J. A. Kelly, the bombardier; Sgt. J. T. Ross, engineer; Sgt. Gordon F. Lewis, radio; Sgt. Maurice Steinhart, belly turret gunner; Sgts. Donald E. Williams and Theodore E. Harkin, waist gunners; and Sgt. C. A. Fatigati, tail gunner.

The crew clambered aboard the *Wicked WAAC* and Wood climbed into the nose section of the plane and settled into his seat before the metal shelf that served as his on-board desk, behind the bombardier and facing the left wing. This position was in the "greenhouse," the small compartment directly behind the tinted Plexiglas nose of the plane. A dome light was on the ceiling above it, and built into one corner of the table was a magnetic compass. Nearby was a set of instruments for indicating altitude and air speed. The navigator had the responsibility of recording the time, direction, altitude, and air speed so he could keep the pilot and bombardier informed of their location. On the larger-scale maps, an inch passed on the ground every minute of flight, and it kept the navigator busy keeping abreast of their location. One navigator's rule was never to take his finger from the map so he'd not lose track of his last checkpoint.[2]

From reports by other crew members, Wood was also to document damage to the plane and the loss of other planes in their group, recording the times they were lost, their location, and how many crewmen managed to bail out, as well as claims of enemy aircraft downed by his own crew. Keeping these records, and remaining aware at all times of their location, meant the navigator was continually preoccupied with paperwork. If that were not enough, above his desk hung the grips of a .50-caliber machine gun he was to use in the event of "emergencies."

Takeoff. A flare lifted through the air, and coughing exhausts punctuated the air as the engines began to turn, first with a low whine, then with an accelerating roar. The mounting roar of seventy-two 1,200 HP engines made the very earth vibrate far from the hardstands on which the eighteen B-17s were poised to taxi. As mechanics pulled the chocks away from their wheels, the huge aircraft moved slowly from their hardstands into a line leading to the main runway and the takeoff point. Liftoff—after they reached an airspeed of 110 to 120 MPH. The co-pilot retracted the landing gear as quickly as they became airborne, the wheels receding into the inboard engine nacelles with a thump.

Eighteen 306th Fortresses took off, their shadows chasing the aircraft into the sky, and slowly fading as the B-17s climbed ever higher. They assembled high over East Anglia, then followed a course to the southeast that took them past one side of London. Although the mission charts show the course passing over the heart of London, such overflights were forbidden, and they swept past the suburbs of the city, over the site of the Battle of Hastings, and out to sea. The 306th Bomb Group, with the rest of the First Air Division, left England on schedule.

The cliffs of Dover, visible from the left side of the plane, were identifiable only as a thin white line along the coast. The Fortresses crossed the English Channel at Hastings at 22,000 feet and continued into France, passing just east of Paris. Their path carried them over Compiègne, then south of Château Thierry, near which Allied troops had turned the tide against the German armies in World War I. Evasive action was taken over airfields and towns, and the formation "S'd" its way over enemy-held terrain to avoid Flak.

A few miles from Romilly a red flare fired from the combat wing leader indicated the Initial Point (IP), and the wingtips of the B-17s lifted high over the horizon as the planes turned into the bomb run. After the IP, the bomb groups flying in each combat wing began to pull apart, to fly one behind another—as though compressed by an invisible funnel into a line. Each group flew a level course straight to the target so bombardiers could fix the target firmly in their bombsights. The bomb groups were now spaced about two miles apart, one behind the other, so their bombs would be concentrated on the target.

The bombardiers moved a lever below their instrument panel to open the bomb doors. Time seemed to drag on the bomb run, for they had to fly through bursts of Flak from 88-millimeter anti-aircraft guns without deviating from their course. Each burst left an expanding black cloud of turbulence—"iron cumulus"—that jarred the planes passing near or through it. Each burst also threw hundreds of fragments of shrapnel and, when they were near enough, many of them tore into the bodies of the Flying Fortresses and their men. The bombardier peered through the bombsight, which, at this moment, was controlling the flight path of the bomber to the target. Bombs away!

The B-17 trembled as the twelve 500-pound general-purpose bombs dropped from the ship; and, passing over the target, they turned into a heading to return to England. Northeast of Romilly the Fortresses reassembled at the rally point to fly home, retracing their outbound flight back to Thurleigh, reaching the English coast without incident. The mission was flown as planned, but it was after dark and the Fortresses could no longer see one another when they finally touched down.

The Tactical Mission Reports said, afterward: "The entire western half of the target received a heavy concentration of bursts and the available photographs show that hardly an installation in this area escaped direct hits."[3] And the 369th War Diary commented: "The 369th scored direct hits on three of six hangars, as confirmed by photographs. Other groups hit hangars and dispersal areas on the north of the field. Very few (10–15) enemy fighters were seen, and they made only desultory attacks with no damage. The flak was moderate, inaccurate, and very low over the target. Our P-47 support was excellent on the way in, but not observed on the way out."

Ten or fifteen enemy fighter attacks had been made from 5 to 7 o'clock but they all broke away at a distance of 600 to 1,200 yards, for the accompanying fighter support prevented close contact with the 306th group bombers. Some Focke-Wulf 190s fired rockets at them, but seventeen of the eighteen 306th planes effectively bombed the primary target. Six of the 273 Fortresses attacking the target were lost to Flak, but the 306th returned without loss, and not one of the 369th ships was even damaged.

It was an enviable introduction to combat for the freshman flier.

CHAPTER FIVE
LAST OF THE MILK RUNS

The second mission flown by Lieutenant Wood, on September 16, was also carried out with little opposition. Eighteen 306th aircraft led by Captain G. E. Paris took off to bomb the U-boat supply ship in the Loire River at Nantes. The flight plan for the mission was designed to keep the bombers far from the French coast until the target was attacked. The planes were to fly directly southwest, past the ruins of Stonehenge, over the west end of the blue-gray waters of the English Channel and far out to sea, then turn to the south, west of the Brest peninsula, before flying a direct route to Nantes and their target. They were to bomb port installations.

Wake-up, latrine, and coffee with breakfast. Briefing. The big sweat of the day came when the assembled crewmen watched as an intelligence officer pulled the curtain back from the huge wall map of Europe that occupied most of the end of the room. There was a chorus of "Ohs" and "Ahs" (mingled with obscenities when the mission was a tough one) as the men's eyes fell on the target. On this mission Lieutenant Wood returned to George Bettinger's crew, and he was to fly the rest of his short tour of duty with this pilot. No one flew every mission, and when men did fly, it was not necessarily in their regularly assigned plane. There was much moving about of crewmen, in part to see that new arrivals had the opportunity to fly some of their first missions with experienced crews.

First Lieutenant George ("Brute") Bettinger, the twenty-seven-year-old pilot, arrived in England on April 1, 1943, having flown across the Atlantic as Charles T. Schoolfield's co-pilot. His first missions were flown as a co-pilot with a crew commanded by Lieutenant Alphonse M. ("Tex") Maresh. He'd been with Maresh on the Schweinfurt-Regensburg mission on August 17, 1943. Ten days later, on August 27, they bombed a rocket-launching installation in northeastern France, only a few miles inland from Calais.

This was the first Eighth Air Force attack on such sites in Operation NOBALL, and the target was the one at Watten, which was being built to launch V-2 rockets against Britain. The installation consisted of a huge concrete bunker set into the earth. It was called "a mysterious hole in the ground" by crewmen, since they were not privy to its identity. The raid was made before the concrete in the bunker had fully set, and the bombs left such a jumble of twisted steel and concrete that another structure had to be built. Today the installations at Watten are a tourist attraction.

Bettinger became a first pilot in early September. His regularly assigned crew was Abraham Block, co-pilot; Elbert Wood, navigator; and the bombardier and engineer. J. E. Hodge flew several missions with him as engineer, and 2nd Lieutenant Ralph G. K. Beach also flew as bombardier. The men flew together for nearly a month, and became about as familiar as was possible for most aircrews in those days. Navigator Wood faced some difficulties in their first few training missions over East Anglia, until he got his bearings. Densely populated England and western Europe posed problems for him, as it did for other navigators trained in the United States, where checkpoints were more easily identified.

On Bettinger's first (but aborted) combat mission as first pilot he took the co-pilot's seat, which he preferred despite his promotion to first pilot. On their return he asked his new co-pilot to land the aircraft, and the man leveled it off about twenty feet above the ground over the end of the runway. Bettinger snatched away the controls and landed, bouncing several times—with a full bomb load aboard. He then discovered that his co-pilot had little experience landing a B-17: the man had been a co-pilot for an officer who'd been disciplined and was flying a target-towing plane as a punishment. Incensed by the situation, the pilot hadn't permitted his co-pilot to fly the plane.

Since the bombers found that the primary target in the Loire River was obscured, they hit the alternate target, the Château Bougon Airfield south of Nantes, where strike photographs showed a good concentration of bombs on the dispersal area. No enemy aircraft were encountered, although other groups were engaged by Focke-Wulf 190s. All 306th aircraft returned safely to base except one that crash-landed at another base because of a mechanical failure.

The 369th War Diary told it as follows: "Today initiated the series of hunts for the big U-boat supply ship in the Loire River of Nantes. Missions of this kind, although much more difficult, lead to greater enthusiasm than those which call for routine attack of stationary targets. Perhaps it is the targets' mobility that gives the excitement of the chase. It was rumored that this boat, aside from being important for U-boat supply, also carried secret equipment for them. At any rate, clouds and smoke screen obscured the primary object of the chase, and the airfield south of the town was let in for some rather deadly bombing. Flying for the 369th were Captain C. W. Wheeler with Lieutenant Klette (27th mission) as co-pilot (they led the group), and Lieutenants E. M. Murphy, W. H. Lockyear, G. C. Bettinger, R. T. Peters, R. W. Porter, and crews."

On this mission Bettinger was assigned the sixth position in the low group—the least desirable position in the entire wing formation. The plane occupying that position was known as "tail-end" or as "ass-end Charlie," while its squadron flew in "Purple Heart Corner." The latter position was usually rotated among the four squadrons in a group, for it was the most exposed of all of those in the wing to enemy fighter attack.

The weather was turning bad. This was, perhaps, a clue to the nature of the coming winter of 1943–44. As far as flying was concerned, it would be one of the worst recorded in the last century.

For a week, poor weather kept the 306th on the ground, and several missions were briefed and then scrubbed. On September 23, the weather lifted and, for the first time in Eighth Air Force history, two heavy-bomber missions were scheduled to be flown on one day: one in the morning and one in the afternoon, both to Nantes.

Early morning: The crew arrived at the hardstand in darkness, about an hour early, to inspect the B-17. It was the *Wicked WAAC* again. The gunners installed and checked the machine guns, which had been stripped from the bomber after its last mission and cleaned by the ground crews.

Accompanying Bettinger, Block, and Wood were 2nd Lieutenant Curtis L. Dunlap, bombardier; Sgt. V. Barney Stevens, engineer; Sgt. J. T. Ross, radio; Sgt. E. E. Wynn, ball turret gunner; Sgt. Theodore A. Harkin, right waist gunner; Sgt. Donald E. Williams, left waist gunner; and Sgt. Walter W. Lastinger, tail gunner. When the Fortress took off, the gunners crowded into the radio compartment to get their weight at the plane's center of gravity.

The early-morning mission was not without difficulty. "Due to darkness and haze, assembly was extremely difficult, two groups being entirely unable to assemble," it was reported. One of the groups was the 306th, which returned to Thurleigh after having climbed to assembly altitude. The crews remained on standby until early afternoon, when the second mission was dispatched. Bettinger was scheduled to fly the sixth position in the high group, but the post-flight interrogation form placed him in the second position. These forms were filled out by base intelligence officers during the debriefing session that followed this, and every other, mission. The interrogation officer grilled each returning crew on all aspects of its flight before the men were permitted to return to their quarters.

Two air divisions struck Nantes several hours apart. Nantes and other targets in France were being attacked in support of a mock invasion operation, code-named STARKEY, which began in late August. This feigned Allied invasion threat was directed toward the Pas-de-Calais, opposite the most constricted part of the English

Channel. It was part of a larger operation designed to give the Germans the impression that an Allied invasion was being planned for the Continent in 1943, in the hope the Germans would halt further troop movements to Italy and the Soviet Union.

"Today we were off for the big U-boat Mother Ship," the 369th War Diary recorded. "The chase was on again, and everybody felt more confident this time since the crews would naturally be more familiar with the target area. However, Jerry was smart with effective smoke screens that obscured what must have been the target, but good bombing on the airport south of the town helped to ease the frustration of 'missing the boat.'"

Eighteen 306th aircraft led by Captain Paris left Thurleigh, and sixteen of them effectively bombed the north bank of the river fork, dock area, and west end of the island at Nantes. The *Wicked WAAC* carried twelve 500-pound bombs. The post-flight interrogation form states that the bombs walked through the dock area and then through the river, although the bombardier didn't see the last of them strike. Flying for the 369th were Lieutenants Bettinger, C. A. Flannagan, Klette, Lockyear, Porter, and Thomas. Only two Focke-Wulf 190s were seen, and these were driven off by the P-47 escort. Flak, it appears, was moderate to intense and was accurate, in fact damaging eight 306th aircraft. The *Wicked WAAC* sustained minor Flak holes.

Ground crews counted off the planes returning to Thurleigh. Ambulance crews at the ends of the runways returned to quarters when the last plane touched down, and when the time had run out for the return of the one remaining Fortress. Seventeen planes came back—all of them except that of Lieutenant Klette, which crash-landed at another base in England. This was his twenty-eighth mission and, told the 369th War Diary, "unfortunately, the last one for a long time. Attempting to land at the RAF station...for gas, the plane crashed. All reports indicate [it was] a miracle that anyone escaped, but all did, although Klette and Madden were severely, if not critically, injured. The others came out well shaken up, with bruises and scratches. Lieutenant Isaac, their bombardier, who palpitates with energy, said he was going to chapel the next day."

Klette was hospitalized for several months, but he recovered, eventually to complete ninety-one combat missions over Europe, an Eighth Air Force record.

Major Robert C. Williams, 306th Bomb Group Operations Officer, registered a complaint following the dual missions that day: "It is recommended that some notice be taken of the physical and mental condition of flying crews when a mission is contemplated. The crews who flew this mission were up for at least twenty-two hours on this day, made two high-altitude formation flights, ate extremely irregular meals, and, in general, exhausted themselves."

Flying as an aerial gunner with the 351st Bomb Group on this mission was an unusual photographer for an Eighth Air Force documentary film. General H. H. Arnold had assigned the photographer, Captain Clark Gable,[1] to head a special unit that was to produce the documentary, which was to be used to recruit and train aerial gunners. It was not a studio production: it was filmed at bases in England and in combat over occupied Europe. Nantes was Gable's last combat mission as a waist gunner-photographer, ending a five-mission stint that included others over The Netherlands, France, Norway, and Germany. Gable and his film crew returned to the United States in October of 1943 with 50,000 feet of color film. This raw footage was edited into the film *Combat America*; it depicted life in the 351st from training in Colorado to air combat over Europe. The authenticity of the film elevated it appreciably above the majority of such propaganda films being made at the time.

*   *   *

On September 26 the men again stepped out into the dawn from the brightly lit briefing room. Another mission. Navigators picked up their flight plans and maps, while gunners were briefed at another location. Trucks then picked them up for the ride to the hardstands. As they pulled away from the briefing area, the men in the backs of the trucks saw a receding panorama of bicycles by the dozen, leaning against buildings and lying on the ground. Bicycles were everywhere on the base—it was the only way to get around—but they were concentrated in the briefing area during missions.

The crew that disembarked at the hardstand consisted of Bettinger, Block, and Wood, plus Ralph G. K. Beach, the bombardier; Sgt. V. Barney Stevens, radio; Sgt. J. E. Hodge, engineer; Sgt. Maurice Steinhart, ball turret; Sgt. Theodore E. Harkin, right waist; Sgt. Donald E. Williams, left waist; and Sgt. Raymond L. Norris, tail gunner. They again carried twelve 500-pound bombs. Bettinger flew the *Wicked WAAC* in the number-two position in the lead group behind Captain Wheeler, who led the 306th.

The mission of the First Air Division was to bomb shipping in the harbor at Nantes, while the Second Division headed for the Dutch coast to fly a diversion. Assembly occurred without difficulty and the force left England on schedule. There was heavy cloud cover over France, however, and the Nantes force was recalled before it crossed the English Channel. The Second Division also was recalled about two-thirds of the way across the North Sea. It was a disappointing day; the excitement and energy expended in an aborted mission was never appreciated, for it did not count as one of the twenty-five missions one had to make to return to the United States—and reassignment to other and less hazardous duty.

*   *   *

Bad weather over Europe during the fall of 1943 made it impossible, most of the time, to bomb in the clear. For this reason, special radar was being developed to permit bombing through the clouds: "blind bombing." The British had developed a self-contained radar device called H2S, that scanned the ground through the clouds and that permitted a trained operator to read a cathode-ray tube screen in the plane like a map. The lead B-17, or Pathfinder, in a combat wing mission was equipped with this instrument, and the bombers behind it dropped their bombs on its signal. Although Emden was not an especially strategic target, its coastal location made it an ideal one for air crews to polish their training in action, because water appeared clearly in the radar image. It was also a good target simply because of the fact that Emden was a German port. True, it was near the German border, but it permitted the Eighth Air Force to claim it was striking targets within Germany.

September 27: another mission, another briefing. A force of 305 Fortresses was dispatched to Emden to test their skill at blind bombing. The formations spiraled up through the dark clouds, the light increasing until the planes broke out into full, blinding sunlight. In every direction, bombers by the hundreds appeared, wheeled in lazy circles, slowly pulled together, assembled, and tightened into defensive formations. Assembly on this day was exceptionally easy, and a few minutes later the intercom announced, "We're leaving England."

They climbed to bombing altitude over the North Sea, the four 1,200 HP Wright Cyclone engines lifting the B-17s and their crews higher and higher into the chilling stratosphere. At the signal "All stations: test fire guns," the gunners fired their .50-caliber guns into the sea so they knew they would work when needed over enemy territory. Below them was a chaotic landscape of clouds, in which one could simultaneously see gray-limned white canyons, beaches and billows, plains, and ranges—into and through which they would occasionally fly, the turbulence leaving ragged streaks behind the aluminum intruders in this dazzling vista. Overhead the sky was dark blue, turning to light blue on the horizon formed by the cloud cover. The first few rounds of Flak burst to the left of the formation as they passed the Frisian Islands.

Eighteen 306th aircraft, led by Captain David W. Wheeler, bombed Emden through an almost solid cloud cover. Roger A. Freeman, in *The Mighty Eighth*, tells that "There was some confusion in manoeuvering above the overcast at the target approach but the lead combat wing successfully dropped in unison with the Pathfinder from 22,000 feet, the second wing dropping on the smoke markers, while the third found no trace of markers and sought to find worthwhile targets elsewhere."[2] There were no direct attacks on the bombers, although twenty to thirty enemy aircraft were seen in the distance and the P-47 escort engaged them in numerous dogfights. This was the deepest penetration of P-47s to date. Flak was moderate and fairly accurate, but all the 306th planes returned to base. Only one of the Fortresses in the lead group was damaged by Flak.

"P-47 support accompanied [us] all the way—a first for them too—and our group bombed on flares dropped by the Pathfinder force in true RAF style. Probably a good many German cows got blasted out of their complacent pastures, but for first time...we surely gave the Emden area...something to contemplate," related the 369th War Diary. Flying for the 369th were Captain Wheeler and Lieutenants Bettinger, G. S. Holmstrom, Lockyear, Murphy, and Thomas, and crews.

Bettinger flew the *Wicked WAAC* in the second position of the lead group, led by Captain David W. Wheeler. The 306th bombers saw nearly twenty enemy aircraft, but only in the distance. One of them was shot down in flames near the target. The *Wicked WAAC* carried 40 incendiary bombs plus two 1,000-pound bombs mounted under the wings on racks next to the fuselage. The mission was without difficulty for the crew, except there was a malfunction on the return trip: the bomb bay doors would not close. Although the added drag meant they had difficulty maintaining formation speed, they returned to Thurleigh without incident.

The crew on that mission was Bettinger, Block, and Wood, plus 2nd Lieutenant Ralph G. K. Beach, bombardier; J. E. Hodge, engineer; V. Barney Stevens, radio; Maurice Steinhart, ball turret; Theodore E. Harkin, right waist; Donald E. Williams, left waist; and Raymond L. Norris, tail. This raid, although not a successful one, demonstrated that H2S could be effective. There was also no doubt that high-altitude, radar-directed bombing was safer from fighter opposition than visual bombing. Photo reconnaissance later revealed that the formation bombing with H2S was reasonably accurate over Emden, but bombs dropped by other formations fell as far as five miles from the target.

The Emden raid was notable for another reason. It was the first time an objective in Germany was attacked by American bombers with a fighter escort. This was made possible on the P-47s by using small auxiliary wing drop tanks that had been introduced in late July.[3] The Luftwaffe lost some twenty fighters in the engagement. No 306th aircraft were lost.

The Eighth Air Force flew no further missions for five days; when it did so, it was another attack on Emden.

*   *   *

There was more encouraging news from the Italian front, for on October 1 Naples was captured by Allied troops. The southern third of the Italian peninsula had now been wrested from Nazi control, but this feat made little difference to the task still facing the Eighth Air Force.

On October 2 a second and much larger blind-bombing raid on Emden took place. It was Lieutenant Wood's sixth combat mission. Escorting P-47 fighters were again able to accompany the bombers to the target. The fighters managed to keep most of the bombers free from German fighters that rose through the clouds, and the enemy fighters did not press the attack on the bombers. "The two H2S aircraft dispatched both bombed but one release was too early resulting in many bombs dropping short of the target. . . .There was obviously much room for improvement."[4]

Eighteen 306th aircraft, led by Captain Frank M. Kackstetter and Colonel Robinson had taken off. "Results were good according to P.R.U. [Photographic Reconnaissance Unit] reports." As the bomb bay doors opened, the bombs tumbled out, slowly righting themselves as they vanished into the clouds.

In the words of the 369th War Diary, "The mission made use of Pathfinders and dropped bombs on a 10/10 cloud cover. The enemy opposition was meager and inaccurate and [the 369th] had only one attack by an E/A. Bombing on the flares from the formation ahead was relatively easy. . . . Practically all the crews voiced the need of a Pathfinder ship with each wing. There was area fighter support which, luckily, did not have much to do, for enemy reaction was not nearly as strong as observed on the first trip on [September] 27th. Not a single ship in the group was damaged." Flying for the 369th Squadron were Lieutenants Porter, Thomas, Holmstrom, Bettinger, Lockyear, Murphy and their crews. "Practically all the fellows 'enjoyed' this mission, if such a thing can ever be enjoyed." There was no fighter opposition and only light, inaccurate Flak. Only two of the 339 bombers that struck the target failed to return.

Lieutenant R. W. Porter led the group, and Bettinger again flew the *Wicked WAAC* in position six in the low formation, "tail-end Charlie." There was solid overcast and they flew at 23,000 feet. Flak was moderate for the 369th squadron, "but it looked like the wing ahead got hell," said the 369th's diary. The crew: Bettinger, Block, and Wood, plus 2nd Lieutenant Ralph G. K. Beach, bombardier; R. L. Grimm, engineer; Gordon F. Lewis, radio; Maurice Steinhart, ball turret; Theodore A. Harkin, right waist; Linden K. Voight, left waist; and Raymond L. Norris, tail. They carried forty-four 100-pound incendiary bombs.

Landing at Thurleigh, Lieutenant Wood scooped his log, charts, and equipment into a duffel bag and explained his notes to the intelligence officer at the debriefing table. Coffee and a shot of whiskey for the crews followed the interrogation. This raid qualified Wood for the Air Medal. This impressive bronze decoration depicts an eagle diving earthward with two lightning bolts clasped in its talons, suspended by a ribbon of royal blue and gold. The medal was awarded after five combat missions—a decoration that announced the simple fact that one had survived five missions over occupied Europe.

*   *   *

Between October 5 and 12, Lieutenant Wood went to one of the Eighth Air Force Service Command's rest homes at Shaftesbury, in Dorset, southwest of London. Coombe House was a palatial estate that had been appropriated by the Eighth Air Force for this purpose. These hostels, or "flak farms," were for crew members who needed a period of rest away from the stress of combat. The growing intensity of air combat left crews on edge. "Partly," as one British writer observed, "the Americans found the appalling business of watching each other die on daylight sorties more harrowing than the anonymity of [the British] night operations."[5]

Why Wood was chosen to go to Shaftesbury is uncertain, since he'd been on only five easy combat missions, and on a sixth that was aborted. The shallow penetrations of the Continent by his formations had not permitted the Luftwaffe time to assemble large groups of fighters to oppose them.

For any combat crewman, these hostels were pure luxury, "just like being out of the army for a week," he wrote. There they wore casual civilian clothes provided for them, momentarily closeting their uniforms with the silver wings over the blue patch on their blouses that designated an "on combat" status. There was excellent food served with silver on white tablecloths, with eggs and fresh fruit every morning for breakfast. Each morning, wake-up was made by a butler bearing a pot of tea. There were no responsibilities whatsoever.

Returning refreshed to Thurleigh on October 12, Lieutenant Wood and his fellows were cheered at the news that Italy had formally declared war on Germany, thereby joining the Allies as a cobelligerent. The news was welcome indeed: three deep penetrations of German airspace had taken place while Wood was away from Thurleigh and the Eighth Air Force had suffered badly at the hands of the Luftwaffe. The week of October 9 to 14 was, in fact, to become known as "Black Week" as a consequence of the losses suffered on those raids and on Second Schweinfurt. October 13 was to be Wood's last "free" day before becoming a participant in one of the most memorable air battles of all time.

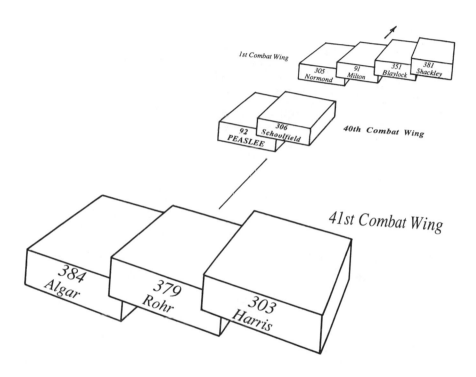

Disposition of the First Air Division bomb groups on entering hostile air space on Second Schweinfurt. The 305th Bomb Group joined the 1st Combat Wing when it could not find the remainder of its own wing. Each bomb group (combat "box") consisted of three squadrons of six planes each. Each wing usually flew at six mile intervals; the Third Air Division was about twenty-five miles behind the First Air Division. Names are those of the leaders of the individual bomb groups.

CHAPTER SIX
SECOND SCHWEINFURT

Three of the four 306th squadrons participated in the Second Schweinfurt raid on October 14, a mission so bitterly fought and ending with such devastating losses to the attacking force that the engagement has become known to the Eighth Air Force as "Black Thursday." Although there were other Allied missions over Europe, using greater numbers of aircraft, and sustaining numerically greater losses, this engagement is generally acknowledged as having been the most savagely fought air battle in history. The magnitude of the German reaction was unprecedented, and the severity with which the pilots executed their mission was devastating. At this time, the Luftwaffe was at its peak strength, and had behind it a magnificent record of past victories to fuel the hunter instincts of the pilots. It was not a propitious time for strategic bombing and, as has been said, the stage was set for tragedy. In military annals, Schweinfurt ceased to be a place name and became, instead, a symbol for disaster. For strategic bombing advocates it was a calamity of lesser proportion than the Battle of Britain had been to the Germans, but one from which, in contrast, the Eighth Air Force eventually could recover.

The task of the mission: to eliminate one of the major sources of ball-bearings, essential to the German war industry. Forty-two percent of these bearings were made in Schweinfurt. Because the

Germans were thought to have almost no reserve supplies, the destruction of Schweinfurt's capacity to make them would be a catastrophic setback for the Nazi war machine.

A successful mission clearly would have shortened the war. This was a heady incentive indeed for the men of the Eighth Air Force. "An ordinary young man is not often told that what he and a few others may do between breakfast and dinner will change the course of world history."[1] Not all of them would be told, although most of them would guess, the probable cost of the mission in men and machines. Everyone by now had heard of Schweinfurt, and the reputation of the "killer town" had been soberly discussed in every barracks. The "double strike" on Schweinfurt and Regensburg on August 17 had cost the Eighth Air Force sixty bombers—a total that, coincidentally, would be matched on Second Schweinfurt.

*   *   *

It was a big operation. The First Air Division, to consist of Fortresses in nine bomb groups, was to lead the mission, which was to reach the Continent ten minutes before the Third Division. The Second Division, with sixty B-24 Liberators, was to fly a more southerly route and reach the target after the Third Division had already bombed Schweinfurt. The return route for all groups was further south, as the weather was expected to deteriorate that afternoon, with low ceilings and poor visibility—which, it was hoped, would handicap the German fighter opposition. Every such handicap they could offer the Luftwaffe would help, for there were discouraging estimates from intelligence: nearly 500 German fighters were thought to be stationed in central and northern Germany, with 200 others in the occupied countries en route to Schweinfurt.

Crews were briefed at 7:00 a.m., and a few hours later a British Mosquito reconnaissance plane dispatched to the target radioed home, "All of central Germany is in the clear." The weather over central Germany was in fact perfectly clear, with almost ideal

visibility. Schweinfurt, an ancient town on the upper reaches of the
Main River in Franconia, northern Bavaria, had a population of
about 65,000, some 17,000 of whom were employed in the ball-
bearings industry. The principal targets of the mission were the
Vereinigte Kugelleger Fabrik (VKF) and Kugelfischer AG (FAG).
Other smaller factories, including those of Fichtel und Sachs Werke,
stood in the suburbs. Remembering the raid on August 17, residents
of Schweinfurt recalled it had been equally clear that day. The term
"Schweinfurt weather" had consequently become so popular that
residents of the town were uneasy about the fine weather on
October 14. When the air raid alarms began sounding that
afternoon in Schweinfurt, no one there was surprised.

*   *   *

The weather in England, however, was terrible. A heavy fog lay on
the land and the damp, murky air moved slowly. The little wind
carried, as usual, the aroma of horses, hay, and the barnyard. Every
farmer had a draft horse, used for light work on the farm, and
Thurleigh, like most other air bases, was surrounded by farmsteads.
The countryside was silent, for there were few tractors nearby, and
there was little automobile traffic off the base.

The call "Board up!" came, and the men, carrying their parachute packs, clambered into the planes through the waist gunner's
compartment. A few minutes before 10:00 a.m., Flying Fortresses
and Liberators at bases scattered across the breadth of East Anglia
started their engines. Takeoff was scheduled to begin at 10:15.

The "Go!" flare arched skyward from the Thurleigh control
tower. Takeoff! Prop wash flattened the grass behind the heavy
bombers as they moved from their hardstands onto the perimeter
track. Because of the heavy fog that weighted down the countryside
that morning, visibility was down to one-quarter of a mile, and the
Fortresses took off at one-minute intervals on full instruments—
instead of the usual thirty-second intervals. With an air speed of
140 MPH, the B-17s wheeled upward through the clouds, using the

needles of their radio compasses to home in on the vertical radio beacons they used to guide them to their assembly points. At 6,500 feet the formations broke into bright sunlight above the clouds over East Anglia, and the groups began to assemble behind their lead planes. It took two hours to assemble the entire wing, and because of the fog all the wings were eighteen minutes late in forming. Bettinger was scheduled to fly the fourth position, directly behind Schoolfield in the lead squadron in the 40th Combat Wing, the second wing in the bomber stream.

The First Division was commanded by Colonel Budd J. Peaslee, who flew as co-pilot with the 92nd Bomb Group's operations officer, Captain James K. McLaughlin, in the commanding aircraft. He was to lead the 383 bombers that were now assembling over England.

Zero Hour: the planes had assembled in formation and now were ready to leave England. There were clouds over England, but the North Sea itself was clear below 10,000 feet.

The Second Division, made up of B-24 Liberators, encountered so much difficulty in assembling that it was forced to cancel its participation in the mission, and twenty-four of its planes were diverted to a secondary target in the Frisian Islands on the coast of Holland.

Save for the B-24s, the raid began auspiciously, at least for the 306th Bomb Group. The eighteen aircraft dispatched by the 306th were led by Captain Schoolfield, an experienced group pilot. Schoolfield's group came into position quickly during assembly. The entire group reached the Continent without an abort, although three planes would shortly turn back less than sixty miles inland from the Dutch coast.

Other groups were not as fortunate. Aborts reduced the number of aircraft in both of the B-17 air divisions. There was another complication. Because of timing, the 305th Bomb Group failed to join the 40th Combat Wing, so one-third of the lead wing's bombers were absent. Peaslee nevertheless opted to continue the mission and, breaking radio silence, radioed the First Combat Wing (behind him) to assume the lead, since wings composed of only two groups were forbidden to enter German airspace for fear such weakness would result in their destruction. He retained his command position in the low group of what now became the second wing in the bomber stream.

*   *   *

The 40th Combat Wing passed over Scole, then flew southeast to the coast of the North Sea and turned east, leaving the English coast at 12:30 p.m. The Luftwaffe day-fighter control organization already knew the approximate size and direction of the striking force, although as yet they had no clue to its target. Fighter units were placed on alert at bases across northwest Europe, and radar stations along the Dutch coast began monitoring the bombers' progress across the North Sea. A little later, German fighters along the coast from Antwerp to Calais took off to intercept them, and were aloft waiting for the bombers when the First Combat Wing entered the Continent. The bomber fleet touched the coast over Walcheren, the southwesternmost island in Holland, about 1:00 p.m. The bombers had now crossed east into another time zone and, under normal circumstances, clocks in Europe would have been an hour later, since both Germany and England were on daylight saving time, or "summer time." For most of the war, however, clocks in England were set ahead two hours in "double summer time," so clocks in both countries registered the same time.

The bomb groups in the First Combat Wing were not flying in their specified positions. Because the 305th Bomb Group had not found the rest of its wing, it joined the First Combat Wing as the low group; when the 381st group arrived, its low position had been taken by the 305th, so it flew as a second high group to the right of the 351st Bomb Group. The Fortieth Combat wing therefore had only two bomb groups instead of three, and a correspondingly smaller number of planes and guns. The Forty-first Combat Wing formed with two high groups, the 303rd flying not as a low group but in a second high position.

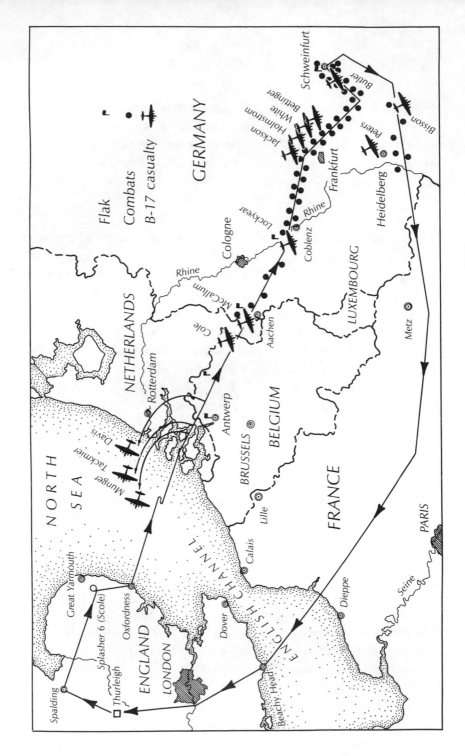

Route of the First Air Division, and aircraft casualties of the 306th Bomb Group on Mission 115. (Base map: track chart of the 306th Bomb Group). (National Archives: Suitland)

By the time they touched the coast of Holland the bomber stream had reached its cruising altitude of about 25,000 feet, and was flying just below a thin layer of scattered cirrus clouds. The soft green, textured fields of the Continent began to roll behind the bombers as they crossed The Netherlands and approached the Belgian border north of Antwerp. The outside temperature was now four degrees below zero, giving them a wind-chill index of sixty degrees below zero in the drafts that now swept through the open waist windows of the Fortresses through which the waist guns protruded. The clouds that had remained below them since they assembled over England disappeared abruptly at the German border.

Fifty P-47 Thunderbolt fighter escorts from the 353rd Fighter Group met the bombers at their rendezvous point over the North Sea and accompanied them to the limit of their range, near the German border at Aachen. At first, the German Messerschmitt Bf-109 fighters directed their attention to the P-47s and tried to scatter them before their depleted fuel tanks made it necessary for them to return to England. One P-47 was shot down, and the American fighter defense did not prevent two B-17s from falling in flames on Belgium as the Thunderbolts, their tanks low on fuel, turned back over Aachen and left for England at 1:33 p.m. The P-47 Jäbos (for *Jägerbomber*, or fighter-bomber), as the Germans called them, had done what they could. The First Division was attacked by fighters almost from the time it entered the Continent; the Third Division, further south, saw only a few enemy fighters until it was well into German airspace.

The moment the P-47s turned for England the massed German fighters directed their full attention to the bombers, and they continued to attack fiercely all the way to Schweinfurt. The "*dicker Hund*" ("Fat Dog," as the bomber stream was dubbed in German fighter slang),[2] suffered heavily at the hands of both fighters and Destroyers all the way to the target. The comment by a bomb group commander regarding First Schweinfurt was to be as appropriate today as it was on that earlier mission: "It was like lining up the cavalry, shooting your way in and then shooting your way out again."[3]

The First Division reached the Continent with 194 bombers. The Third Division, flying thirty miles to the south, did so with a force of 142. Although nearly 383 bombers left England, 92 aircraft aborted before reaching the Continent, and only 257 planes actually penetrated the German border.

"We had no trouble until the P-47's left," Schoolfield later said, "then all hell broke loose. Between the Rhine and the target our formations were attacked by at least three hundred enemy aircraft. Rockets mounted under the wings of enemy aircraft fired into our tight defensive formation caused the highest rate of casualties. The crews described the scene as similar to a parachute invasion, there were so many crews bailing out."[4] At one time there were as many as 150 parachutes in the air. The First Division came under attack by perhaps 250 to 300 German fighters, principally Focke-Wulf 190s and Messerschmitt Bf-109s, in one continuous air battle across central Germany. They were joined by Messerschmitt Bf-110 Destroyers, who kept beyond the range of the bombers' machine guns and fired rockets into the Fortresses from behind them. White streaks from tracers and the crimson trails of air-to-air rockets crisscrossed the sky.

James E. Harris, flying with Butler in the 367th, the low squadron of the 306th, reported that "The German fighters hit us as soon as our escort left. I had never seen so many enemy fighters and planes of various types: The single-engine FW-190s and Me-109s rolled through the Bomb Groups, twin-engine and even sea planes lay out beyond our range and lobbed rockets at us, as bombers dropped aerial bombs from above into our formations. . . .The intercom was bedlam with crew members calling out fighter attacks. It got so bad that it didn't do any good to call them out."[5] His was the eleventh bomber of the 306th to be shot down.

The most compelling account of the air battle, however, was composed by Colonel Budd J. Peaslee, flying as the group commander in the low group immediately to the left of Schoolfield's

306th group. It is told in Robert E. O'Hearn's 1984 *In My Book You're All Heroes*: "Suddenly, the . . . air waves became a bedlam of excited voices calling 'Bogies! Bogies! —Hostiles! Hostiles!' There was little need for the alerting cries, for a constant vigilance was key to survival for airmen. Radio chatter increased in intensity and became a confusing jumble of sound as the callers throughout the bomber formations tried to warn their comrades of the approach of enemy fighters. 'Hostiles at 6 O'Clock. Hostiles at 9 O'Clock. Hostiles at 3 O'Clock!' Radio discipline ceased to exist for a brief period until the attacks were launched and until, in truth, the Heavens erupted and were filled with tumult and shouting. The enemy had surrounded us and the battle was enjoined.

"The enemy fighters came in from every direction. Most terrifying were the head-on attacks that seemed to materialize from nowhere and were first observed as continuous flashes in the sky ahead as the Germans opened fire on our compact defensive formations, to disrupt and weaken our mutually protective fire screens and to divert us from our objectives. The great military advantage lay with the Germans, who had overwhelming numbers, at times outnumbering us ten to one, and great speed, exceeding that of the bombers by more than 100 miles per hour. It was estimated that more than 800 fighters rose on this occasion to deny us passage. The fire of our defensive guns was almost ceaseless and in many cases our ammunition became exhausted before we reached the targets. To the everlasting credit of the bomber crews these vicious tactics failed with a completeness that must have been disheartening to the attacking fighters. The bombers paid a grievous toll for their steadfastness in dead and wounded, but their determination and discipline prevailed and formations bored on towards Schweinfurt and the vital ball-bearing complex of the Third Reich.

"The combat was continuous as the opposing legions moved eastward high above the hinterland. The single-engine Messerschmitt 109s and the Focke-Wulf 190s with their great speed and maneuverability struck us from our flanks, diving inward and through the formations with blazing guns, then climbing back above us to repeat their asp-like attacks. The twin-engine Heinkel 111s, like hyenas, approached from the rear to launch their devastating eight-inch rockets that were frightful to behold as they exploded with an angry red core of flame and a massive, shapeless blob of smoke. The Germans initiated . . . their soul-shattering head-on attacks passing under and through our formations.

"As the battle progressed, the hurts became more apparent. Throughout the formations bombers began to falter and fall behind or sink towards the earth far below. Some fuel tanks were ruptured and the burning, volatile gas force fed by the wind velocity ate through the soft metals of the aircraft structures, destroying aerodynamic qualities that kept them aloft. From some of these bombers blossomed parachutes in quick succession, and on rare occasions all ten of the crewmen would float down towards the German Prisoner of War Camps. From others, when the machine died in violence, the crews were unable to reach the exits and became an indistinguishable part of the rubble when the bomber exploded on impact. . ."[6]

Eight 306th Bomb Group Flying Fortresses were shot down between Antwerp and the outskirts of Schweinfurt.

*   *   *

The German fighters and Destroyers were heavily armed with both machine guns and 20-millimeter cannons. In addition, they carried air-to-air rockets. These eight-inch (21-centimeter) rockets were used for the most part on twin-engined Junker 88s and Messerschmitt Bf-110s, and also on some single-engine Focke-Wulf 190s and Messerschmitt Bf-109s. Four rockets were electrically discharged from beneath the wings of twin-engined planes, and two from single-engine aircraft. This aerial rocket was adapted from a widely used *Werfer Granate* infantry mortar, manufactured by Mauser.

These deadly missiles were carried in launch tubes (German

pilots called them "stovepipes") suspended beneath the wings of the aircraft. Each 250-pound, spin-stabilized rocket carried a 90-pound warhead and had a velocity of more than 1,000 feet per second. The ideal mode of attack was to fly behind the bombers out of the 1,000-yard effective range of their machine guns, and launch the rocket into the bomber formations. The missiles were fused to detonate at a predetermined range of 600 to 1,200 yards. Although they could not be aimed with any precision—the German aircraft were simply "pointed" toward the enemy when the rockets were launched—the tight B-17 combat boxes were broken up when these missiles exploded among them, making the individual bombers easier targets for the standard fighter interceptors.

The rockets produced explosive bursts two to four times as large as the 88-millimeter Flak. Their path was marked by a long, luminous crimson streak, and the black burst of smoke left when it detonated had a dirty-red center. Only one direct strike was usually needed to destroy a bomber.[7] In contrast, the Mauser 20-millimeter cannon on the German fighters had 200 rounds, and it took 20 to 25 hits with these shells to bring down a B-17.

*   *   *

The most intensive Flak of the mission was the barrage that hit the bombers at the outskirts of Schweinfurt. It was almost welcome, for the bomber crews expected the enemy fighters to pull away from the bombers, and avoid destruction by their own guns. Wrong! The German fighters continued their attacks as savagely as ever, and even over Schweinfurt the First Division bombers were under attack by as many as forty to fifty enemy aircraft. The seven remaining bombers of the 306th joined with the remnants of the 92nd Bomb Group for the bomb run, and dropped their bombs successfully despite the continued attacks, placing most of their 1,000-pound bombs on or near the Mean Point of Impact at the target.

As the returning fliers left their target they turned, first south, and then west, for the flight home. Each crew that was not still fighting off German attacks could see roiling billows of black smoke rising over a mile in the air over Schweinfurt, where the destruction was heavy even in the suburbs. As rewarding as the sight behind them might have been to the embattled men, it was canceled by the view out their right windows: as far as they could see were dozens of columns of black, turgid smoke blooming upward from the pyres of downed B-17s. These dismal flares marked, on the soil of Europe, the route to Schweinfurt that had been depicted by the yarn on the briefing room maps at bases throughout England only a few hours earlier. Until the target was reached, however, almost every Fortress that went down "was still pointing its nose at the target,"[8] including Lieutenant Butler's B-17, shot down on the bomb run about four minutes outside Schweinfurt. Two more Fortresses of the 306th were lost after hitting the target: those piloted by Bisson and Peters. The remaining five 306th bombers returned to England, although Bickett crashed on landing and the other four planes suffered varying degrees of battle damage. The net loss or damage to the group: one hundred percent.

*   *   *

This was the second trip to Schweinfurt for the 369th Bomb Squadron. According to the 369th War Diary: "On the first raid of 17 August, 1943, the 306th put up 30 A/C [aircraft]. A great aerial battle developed, but splendid formation flying and general luck brought them all back, although other groups in the last Bombardment Wing lost 36 planes. The second raid has spelled out an entirely different story for us. . . . Between the Rhine and the Target (right after the P-47 escort left) the formation was attacked by 300 enemy aircraft (mostly using Focke-Wulf 190s, Messerschmitt Bf-109s and 110s, and Junker-88s), using deadly rocket tactics." The 369th lost Lieutenants Bettinger, Holmstrom, Lockyear, and Peters, and their crews. "Returning for the 369th were only Captain Schoolfield, Lieutenant Noack and their crews, whose claims on E/A run 3-1-4 [three confirmed destroyed, one probably destroyed, and four damaged]. We look forward to the inevitable replacement crews. May they be the equal of these good fellows who have gone. And may their luck be better."

The 306th Bomb Group alone lost ten of the sixty bombers downed over Europe that day, more than half of the eighteen planes that left Thurleigh. Three planes returned early, and seven bombed Schweinfurt, but only five of them completed the mission. The ten bombers that did not return meant that exactly one hundred 306th men were killed or captured—one-sixth of those lost on Second Schweinfurt. Two-thirds of those one hundred men survived the day; fully one-third of them were killed in action. The losses of the 306th, severe as they were, were exceeded by the 305th Bomb Group. Only two of its bombers returned.

Despite these heavy losses, the target was bombed by 228 Flying Fortresses. Although the damage appeared to be extensive at the time, in the long run the mission had no decisive effect on the manufacture of ball-bearings. One of its most visible effects was the realization, by the German people, that the massed American daylight bomber formations of August 17 and October 14 meant that most of the cities in Germany were now targets that could suffer the same fates as London and Coventry.

Altogether, sixty American bombers were shot down and their crews lost over enemy territory; another five were abandoned or crash-landed when they returned to England; and others were so badly damaged that they were suitable only for salvage. In purely monetary terms, the Eighth Air Force expended more than $21 million dollars in aircraft and equipment that afternoon, to say nothing of its investment in highly trained flight personnel. But the loss on Black Thursday went much deeper than the loss of the bombers and their crews: air superiority was temporarily lost to the Luftwaffe, and it was the death of unescorted daylight bombing over Germany. The eight-hour, forty-minute strike so reduced the Eighth Air Force that no further missions to the heart of Germany were possible until early 1944. Schweinfurt was not visited again by the Eighth Air Force until February 24, with the loss of another forty-four American bombers.

"On this memorable day," Adolf Galland, commander of the Luftwaffe fighter forces said, "we managed to send up almost all the fighters and destroyers which were available for the defense of the Reich, and in addition a part of the fighters of the 3rd Air Fleet, France. All together 300 day fighters, 40 destroyers, and some night fighters took part in this air battle which for us was the most successful one of the year 1943. We were able to break up several bomber formations and to destroy them almost completely. . . . On the German side about 35 fighters and destroyers were lost."[9] Many others were, of course, damaged. If the intelligence accumulated by the Eighth Air Force overestimated the number of German fighters available, the B-17 gunners also overestimated the 91 German fighters they claimed to have destroyed on Second Schweinfurt. German newspapers realistically and properly claimed the battle a Luftwaffe victory, quite opposed to General Henry H. Arnold's announcement to the Allied press on October 18 that "Now we have got Schweinfurt!"

CHAPTER SEVEN

THE DESTRUCTION OF THE
WICKED WAAC

The men in the *Wicked WAAC* were only vaguely aware of many of the tactical details presented in the preceding chapter. They had two simple missions that day: to bomb the primary target if possible and, even more desirable, to return to base. Among most bomber crews there was much skepticism about the possible success of either goal. The fact that the 306th had lost not one of its thirty bombers on First Schweinfurt was regarded as a lucky fluke that was unlikely to be repeated.[1]

The ten crewmen who climbed aboard the *Wicked WAAC* on Black Thursday for the strike on Schweinfurt provided a cross section of America, coast to coast. Four and a half hours later, these young men from New England, the Midwest, the West, and California were to join hundreds of others in the running air battle with the Luftwaffe across the skies of Central Europe.

1st Lt. George C. Bettinger, Pilot	Alhambra, CA
2nd Lt. Abraham Block, Co-pilot	Chicago, IL
2nd Lt. Elbert S. Wood, Navigator	Cody, NE
2nd Lt. Leland A. Dowden, Bombardier	Sacramento, CA
S/Sgt. Samuel F. Gerking, Engineer	Hood River, OR
S/Sgt. Gordon F. Lewis, Radio Operator	Centerville, MA
T/Sgt. Elmer W. Mills, Ball Gunner	Bronx, NY

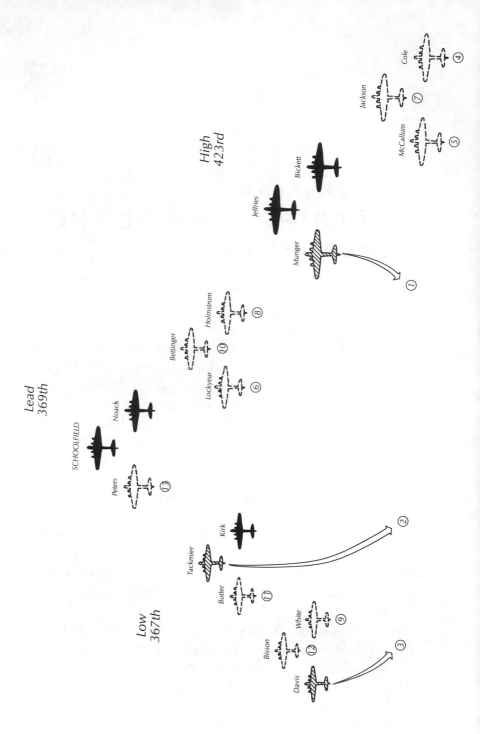

Formation diagram for the 306th Bomb Group on Second Schweinfurt.
Solid black = aircraft that returned to base after bombing;
hatched = aircraft that returned early; dashed outline = aircraft shot down.
Numbers denote the sequence in which the planes left formation
or were shot down.

S/Sgt. James F. Montana, R. Waist Gunner   Chicago, IL
S/Sgt. Donald E. Williams, L. Waist Gunner   Wayne City, IL
S/Sgt. Linden K. Voight, Tail Gunner   Denver, CO

Second Schweinfurt was Bettinger's eighteenth mission. Block, Wood, Williams, and Voight were the only regular crewmen that day. Alternates filled the remaining positions. The formation diagram called for Bettinger to fly the lead squadron in the fourth position.

On the morning of October 14, twenty-six-year-old 2nd Lieutenant Leland A. Dowden was called to report to the briefing room and, upon arrival, was told that the bombardier scheduled for one of the crews had been put on the sick list and that he was to replace him. It was Dowden's second mission: his first had been to the harbor at Gdynia, Poland, on October 9, five days earlier. At the briefing all the crew were strangers to him except Gerking, who was Dowden's regular engineer on another crew. This was normal procedure. It was a general practice that new crews were split up for the first few missions so the men could fly with experienced crews. The sick bombardier, who usually carried a toy bear—or monkey—for good luck, decided to stand down and not fly the Schweinfurt mission. Such tokens meant little to Williams, who said, "I'd rather have had another Flak jacket than a good luck charm."

Staff Sergeant Samuel Gerking, called by Donald Williams a "big lumberjack type" native of Oregon, stood in for the top turret gunner on the *Wicked WAAC*. Gerking was the new engineer on Dowden's regular aircraft, piloted by William B. Hilton. Second Schweinfurt was his first and last mission. Many men arrived at a base, settled into their barracks, flew their first mission a day or so later, and were replaced, as Donald Williams phrased it, "before they realized they'd been in England."

Staff Sergeant and radioman Gordon F. Lewis had participated in the July 24, 1943, raid on Heroya, Norway, when his plane, flown by Lieutenant Alfonse H. ("Tex") Maresh, was so damaged by Flak that it ditched in the ocean near Cromer on its return.

Staff Sergeant James F. Montana, a twenty-seven-year-old from Chicago, was the right waist gunner, but he was usually assigned to the *Wahoo*. This plane, flown by Lieutenant Robert P. ("Rip") Riordan, carried nose art depicting an Indian holding Hitler's scalp and brandishing a tomahawk. Montana was a good singer with a good voice, and often burst into song in the plane. Second Schweinfurt was his sixteenth mission. The left waist gunner, Staff Sergeant Donald E. Williams, was a twenty-two-year-old from Illinois, and part Comanche Indian.

Twenty-two-year-old Technical Sergeant Elmer Warren ("Pete") Mills was on his twenty-fifth—and last—mission. Mills gained the only fighter claim for the August 12, 1943, raid on Gelsenkirchen[2]—a Messerschmitt Bf-109 destroyed. He'd volunteered for the October 14 mission before he knew what the target was to be. Although he desperately wanted to back out when he learned of their destination, he couldn't: "My pride just wouldn't let me." He'd flown on the August 17, 1943, Schweinfurt-Regensburg mission, so he had no illusions about the difficulties they faced.

Staff Sergeant Linden K. ("Lin") Voight, thirty-five years old, was the tail gunner and the "old man" of the crew, being at least ten years older than the rest of the men. He'd been awarded a Purple Heart in July 1943. Like Lewis, he had participated in the July 24 raid on Norway. When he suffered Flak wounds on the August 27, 1943, raid on the V-2 rocket installation at Watten, France, he was recommended for a second Purple Heart.

*   *   *

They lifted off at 10:25 a.m. The wing tips dissolved into the mist over Thurleigh and they climbed through the clouds to join their group and formation without difficulty. All the Fortresses of the 306th Bomb Group remained in tight formation until they entered the Continent. Shortly after entering Holland, however, mechanical difficulties forced two 306th planes to turn back for England. First

Above: Contrails forming behind a high-flying B-17; note the spiral pattern left by propeller turbulence. (Courtesy of Gerald R. Massie)

Below: Coombe House, the Eighth Air Force's rest home at Shaftesbury, where Lieutenant Wood spent the week before Black Thursday. Shaftesbury is in southern England a few miles west of Stonehenge.

BREAKFAST 0615	BRIEFING 0715	STATIONS 1005	TAXI 1015	
CAMERAS		TAKE OFF 1025	ASSEMBLE AT	FT
LUNCH	SANDWICHES	RADIO CHECK	TO AT 1130 HOURS
CONVOYS		REND Thur	AT 1132 AT 14,000 FT
		REND	AT AT FT

SPARES 074 : 145 : 714 :	: :		:	:
OXYGEN R : D : D :	: :		:	:
DISP'L 24 : 48 : 3 :	: :	Thur	: 1132	: 14,000
GROUP C.O. Schoolfield		Stoney Stratford	: 1140	: 14,000
GROUP DEPUTY Tackmier		Daventry	: 1148	: 14,500
GROUP DEPUTY		Spaulding	: 1206	: 18,000
CLIMB AT 150 AT 200 FPM		Splasher #6	: 1222	: 21,000
CRUISE AT 155 AT 24,000 FT		Oxfordness	: 1230	: 21,000
CMB AT 150 AT 24,000 FT		5140-0340E	: 1252	: 24,000
RETURN AT 155 AT 21,000 FT		5130-0415E (P-47)	: 1259	:
DESCEND AT 165 AT 500 FPM		5057-0608E	: 1323	:
SPLASHER NO. 9 LET DOWN 315 DEGREES		5033-0707E	: 1336	:
ALTIMETERS 29.92 TOP TANKS yes		5023-0844E	: 1355	:
ZERO HOUR 1230 BOMB INT. Minimum		IP 4948-0955E	: 1413	:
AUDIT FLASHING LETTERS		TARGET	: 1418	:
92 GP LEADS 305-306		4954-1033E	: 1422	: 22,000
40 CW LEADS 1st, 41st.		4925-1022E	: 1433	: 21,000
92 GP YY PERIOD 0700-1300:1300-1900		4913-0822E	: 1500	:
305 GP RG FLARE RY : GG		4858-0602E	: 1533	:
306 GP RY ANSWER P : I		4904-0358E	: 1601	:
GP CHALLENGE L : B		4940-0230E (Spits)	: 1623	:
FIGHTER SUPPORT 1 gp. P-47 5130-0415 to max		5007-0128E	: 1642	:
range. 1 gp P-38 area near Flushing on way in.		Beachy Head	: 1704	: 10,000
1 gp. P-47 4908-0355 on way out. 4 sq. Spit		Base	: 1743	:

IX 4940-0230 to mid-channel. 4 gp. P-47 and
8 sq. Spit to cover 2 & 3 ATF in and out.
OTHER EFFORTS 3rd Div. depart Clacton at
1230 to 5122-0321 to 5038-0602 to 4935-0707 to
4948-0955 to target. Ret same as us. 3rd Div.
departs Orfordness at 1300 same route as us.

START ENGINES
STAND BY MESSAGE
DELAY TAKE OFF
SCRUB
ABANDON

FIGHTERS	HAYBANK (47's)	DUNLOP (Spits)
BOMBERS	PHONEBOX 2	BUCKSHOT 1
M.S.C.	WARMSUN	SPICECAKE
Air Commander ROSE BUD		

Mission 115 orders for October 14, 1943.
(National Archives: Suitland)

A Messerschmitt Bf-110 Destroyer of Staffel 5 of II./ZG 76 in 1943/1944, armed with 21 centimeter rocket launchers. (Courtesy of Herbert Kist)

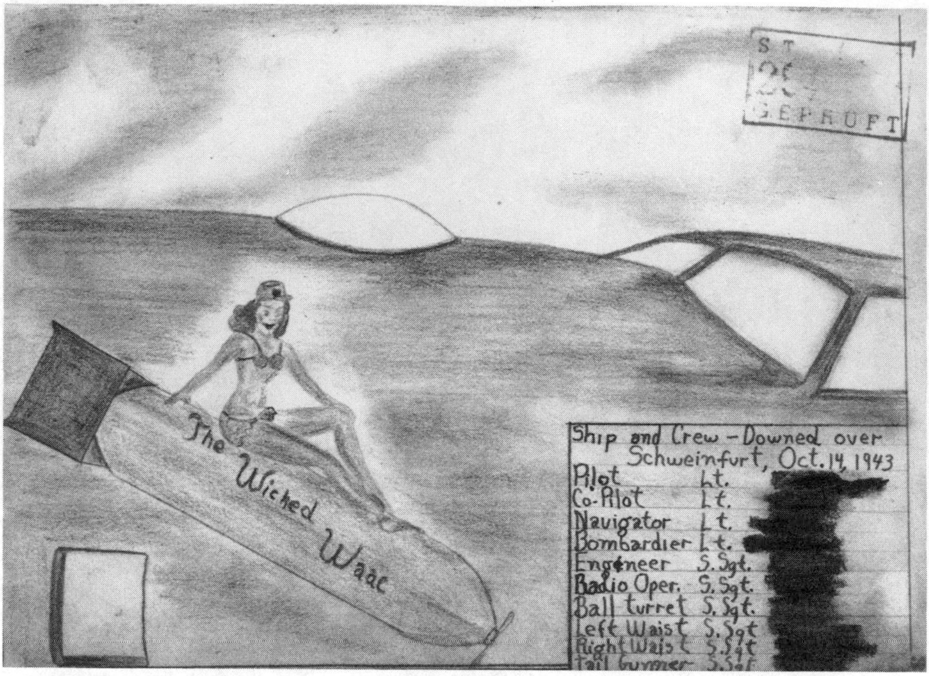
GEPRUFT
The Wicked Waac
Ship and Crew – Downed over Schweinfurt, Oct. 14, 1943
Pilot Lt. [redacted]
Co-Pilot Lt.
Navigator Lt.
Bombardier Lt.
Engineer S. Sgt.
Radio Oper. S. Sgt.
Ball turret S. Sgt.
Left Waist S. Sgt
Right Waist S. Sgt
Tail Gunner S. Sgt

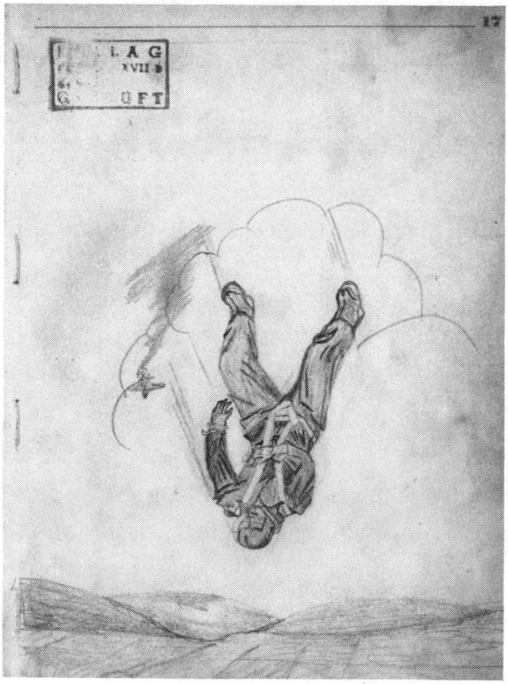
17
XVII B

Although there are no known photographs of the *Wicked WAAC*, this sketch by an anonymous artist at Stalag XVII-B, from the POW diary of Donald E. Williams, at least preserves a record of the nose art. The names of the crew were scratched out for security reasons. Note the German censors' stamp on this, and on the depiction of a "bailout in Bavaria," at left. (Courtesy of Donald E. Williams)

STAND BY FOR BROADCAST

MOL TO GUN KBM THU TO POD

XM

USLIST P V BMP 53 -OP-

T USLIST P

FROM COMBOVDIV ONE 132315A

TO: ALL GROUPS EXCEPT ALC, ALL CW'S

SECRET SENT IN CLEAR AUTH. MAJ. RYAN 1BD O-709-E.

   TO ALL LEADERS AND COMBAT CREWS. TO BE READ AT
BRIEFING.

   THIS AIR OPERATION TODAY IS THE MOST IMPORTANT AIR
OPERATION YET CONDUCTED IN THIS WAR. THE TARGET MUST BE
DESTROYED. IT IS OF VITAL IMPORTANCE TO THE ENEMY. YOUR
FRIENDS AND COMRADES THAT HAVE KQSXXA BEEN LOST AND THAT WILL
BE LOST TODAY ARE DEPENDING ON YOU. THEIR SACRIFICE MUST
NOT BE IN VAIN. GOOD LOXXX LUCK, GOOD SHOOTING, AND GOOD
BOMBING. ANDERSON. COMBOMDIV ONE.
AS

JG B

THU R.........132345A HERSMAN K

Teletype message from Brig. General Frederick L. Anderson at Bomber
Command, sent to all Eighth Air Force bomb groups participating in Second
Schweinfurt. This message, as received by the 306th Bomb Group, was read
following the crew briefings. There is some speculation that this "in clear"
message was somehow communicated to the Luftwaffe, although this is
denied by the Germans.

Badger Beauty V on October 4, 1943. (Courtesy of Squadron Signal Publications)

B-17s of the 483rd Bomb Group. (Courtesy of Squadron Signal
Publications)

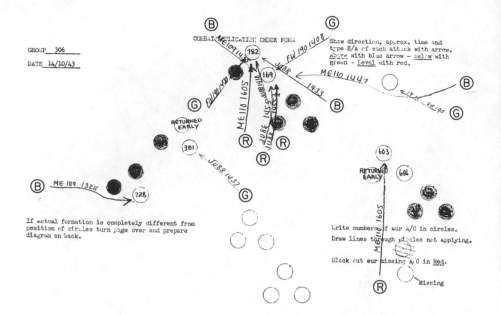

COMBAT DUPLICATION CHECK FORM

GROUP 306

DATE 14/10/43

Show direction, approx. time and type E/A of each attack with arrow. Above with blue arrow - below with green - Level with red.

RETURNED EARLY

If actual formation is completely different from position of circles turn page over and prepare diagram on back.

RETURNED EARLY

Write number of our A/C in circles.
Draw lines through circles not applying.

Block out our missing A/C in Red.

Missing

Above: Combat Duplication Check Form for the 306th Bomb Group, showing group losses and enemy attacks. These forms were compiled by intelligence officers from information obtained during post-mission debriefings. Labels for B=blue, G=green, and R=red have been added. (National Archives: Suitland)

Below: A B-17 not yet tested in battle. (Courtesy of Squadron Signal Publications)

Above: A Flying Fortress fulfilling its intended purpose. (Courtesy of Squadron/Signal Publications)

Below: 306th Bomb Group formation diagram for October 14, 1943. (National Archives: Suitland)

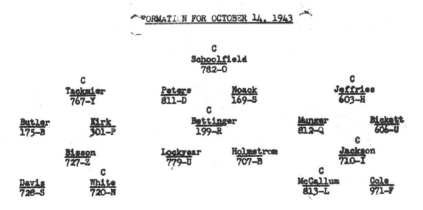

FORMATION FOR OCTOBER 14, 1943

C
Schoolfield
782-O

C   C
Tackmier   Peters   Noack   Jeffries
767-Y   811-D   169-S   603-H

                                  C
Butler   Kirk   Bettinger   Munger   Rickett
175-B   301-P   199-R   812-Q   606-U

                                                                 C
Bisson   Lockyear   Holmstrom   Jackson
727-Z   779-U   707-B   710-I

           C   C
Davis   White   McCallum   Cole
728-S   720-N   813-L   971-F

C above pilot's name indicates camera on ship.

"And There We Were." A light-hearted version of the attack on the *Wicked WAAC*, drawn for Donald Williams by fellow POW George W. Soell at Stalag XVII-B. The aircraft serial number on the tail is not the correct one. (Courtesy of Donald E. Williams)

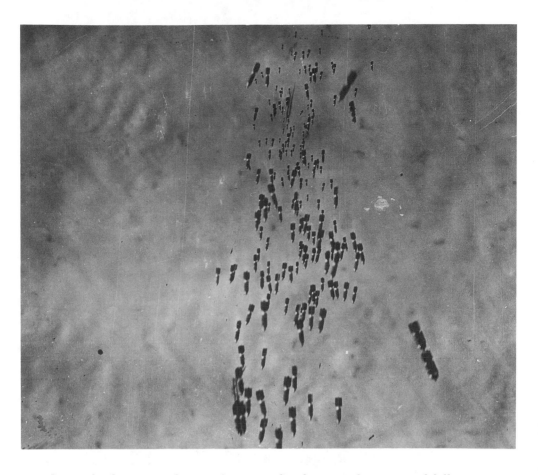

Above: The destructive charges of an entire bomb group plunge toward full cloud cover. Each B-17 carried twelve such 500-pound bombs. (Courtesy of Mrs. Gerald E. Massie)

Below: Wreckage of the *Fichtel und Sachs Werke* plant in Schweinfurt after the air strike on October 14, 1943. (Courtesy of Hans-Heiri Stapfer)

INTERROGATION FORM

SQUADRON ~~367 XXX~~ 369 ~~XXXX~~   A/C Number 782   Letter 0   Date 14/10/43

Bomb Load 6 x 1000 H.E. Incend.

Time Took Off ~~1925~~ 1025   Time Landed 1755

<table>
<tr><td colspan="2">Position in Formation</td></tr>
<tr><td></td><td>⊗</td></tr>
</table>

1. HOT NEWS to be phoned in? Yes No
   Details:

Position in Formation

```
    X        X  X        X
 X  X     X     X     X  X
    X        X  X     X  X
 X  X     X     X     X  X
    X                    X
```

CREW: Give Rank and Initials

Friendly A/C in any kind of distress?
(Give position, time, altitude, full
details)

See attached sheet

Capt. C.T. Schoolfield	Pilot ✓
Capt. C.E. Flannagan	Co-P ✓
Lt. D.B. Dash ✓	
Lt. J.B. Mazanek	Nav. ✓
Capt. F.A. Evans	Bomb. ✓
T/Sgt. M.A. Narum	Radio
T/Sgt. J.C. Stoner ✓	Top T.
T/Sgt. B.A. Hardy ✓	Ball T.
S/Sgt. B.H. Perlmutter ✓	R. Waist
S/Sgt. R.J. Conley ✓	L. Waist
Lt. C.L. Dunlap	Tail G. ✓

2. TARGET ATTACKED:

   (Primary)   Time: 1445

   Alternate   Height: 22500

   Last Resort   Heading 45°
   (circle)
   Duration Bomb Run:

                  40 sec

3. Number of BOMBS dropped on target: 6   Jettisoned: Returned: Abortive:

4. Observed RESULTS OF BOMBING: (for this plane or others)

   Own Bombs:

   Ours of 92nd

   Other Bombing: *light in town center - fires &
   large smoke col. in target area   2000 FEET*

5. Any Photographs taken: (Yes) No?   Any Nickels: Yes (No)
                                           Number boxes dropped ___
                                           Number boxes returned ___

6. GROUND TARGETS ATTACKED BY GUNFIRE AND RESULTS:

7. ROUTE: (If different than ordered) (If ABORTIVE give time, place,
          height of turn; reason for returning early; and disposition
          of bombs)
   As briefed over Germany

8. WEATHER: (If it affected mission) *Clear over target*

9. FLAK: Encountered on way out, at target and on way home.

<table>
<tr>
<th>Time</th><th>Place</th><th>Height
of
A/C</th><th>Type (light,
heavy), intense,
moderate or
slight.</th><th>Color
of
bursts</th><th>Location
Bursts in re-
lation to A/C</th><th>Accuracy</th>
</tr>
<tr><td>Intermittant</td><td colspan="3">thru-out route starting at</td><td></td><td></td><td></td></tr>
<tr><td>Antwerp -</td><td colspan="3">slight not too acc.</td><td></td><td></td><td></td></tr>
<tr><td>Target</td><td></td><td></td><td>mod -</td><td>black</td><td>all right in the town</td><td>very acc.</td></tr>
</table>

Crew observations about Flak:

2 red burst just at French coast

border in - fighters missed jumped wing behind

This page and facing page: Interrogation Form (front and back) for Captain
Charles T. Schoolfield, 306th Bomb Group leader on October 14, 1943.
(National Archives: Suitland)

10. ENEMY FIGHTER OPPOSITION?

Everything — mostly twins

250 - 300 plus.
(Estimated total number of E/A seen)   (Types)

14:30 just before Achen - near ~~Sta~~ Ludwigshaven
(Location and length of fight)

no attacks from front, both S/E & T/E pressed attacks
T/E E/A shot rockets. T/E shooting machine
guns to rear.— most attacks came from
between 4 & 8 o'clock - E/A cued up.
(Tactics of E/A)

Me 110 solid black, silver, yellow & greenish
wings body
blue
yellow nose
(Color, markings, etc. of E/A)

normal evasive
action
(Our defensive action)

looked like camouflage during firing shooting rockets

CLAIMS

DESTROYED   3
PROBABLY   1
DAMAGED   1
(Fill out immediately
separate CLAIM FORM for
each claim.

11. FIGHTER SUPPORT

Good going in, none seen
coming out (would min late
coming out)

12. OBSERVATIONS: Give TIME, PLACE, HEIGHT (List any observations of military
importance such as balloons, decoys, dummies, camouflage, smoke screens, enemy
signals; activity at airdromes, ports, waterways, roads, railroad yards; concentrations of vehicles, troops, vessels; landmarks, new enemy installations,

Ludwigshaven smoke screens, several unidentified
observed - very quick action in one town - resulting
in an excellent smoke screen

13. INCIDENTS TO FRIENDLY A/C: (If one of our A/C lost, state whether by A.A.,
E/A Action, Accident or Undetermined Cause)

B17's most with rockets

14. INJURIES TO CREW: (Give name, position in A/C, type of injury, how
received, PLACE and TIME.)

Hand blown off by 20 mm - hit flak suit & exploded
T/S R.J. Conley - waist - gunner - before I.P.

15. DAMAGE TO A/C: (Briefly)

numerous flak hole, one brush by

16. TECHNICAL FAILURES: rocket.

17. CREW COMMENTS: (Any unusual incidents? Any suggestions?)

R.J. Conley - shot down fighter after hand blown
off.

S-2 OFFICER R Skalak   TIME COMPLETED

Need fighter support against rockett ships.

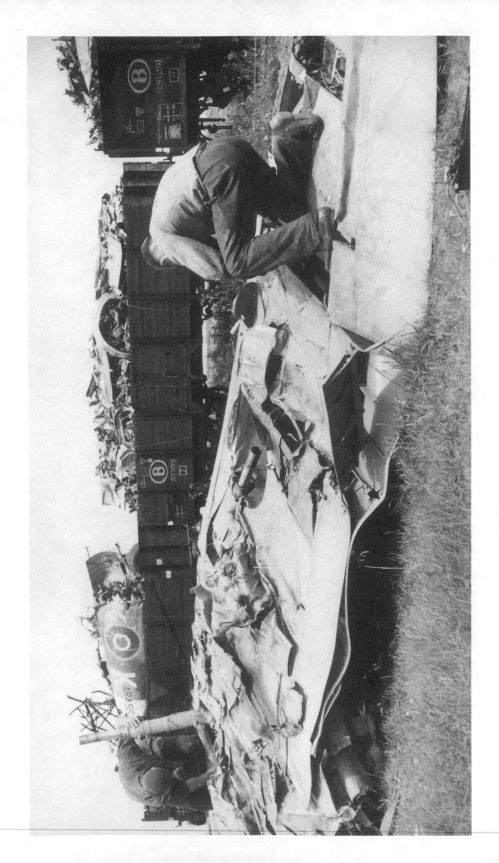

Facing page: Scrap from fallen Allied Aircraft arrives at a salvage yard. Since the railroad cars belong to the Belgian railroad system, the yard is probably the one at Utrecht, in The Netherlands.

Below: Part of *Fightin' Pappy,* a B-17 of the 379th Bomb Group, being readied for further dismantling at the Nanterre salvage yard in the suburbs of Paris.
(Photographs courtesy of Hans-Heiri Stapfer)

A worker removing the wing of a B-17 in the salvage yard at Nanterre in late 1943. (Photograph courtesy of Hans-Heiri Stapfer)

Clarence E. Munger, and then William J. Tackmier, dropped out of formation because of supercharger malfunctions. They couldn't maintain speed and stay with the formation. A few minutes later, as the bombers passed into Belgian airspace, Zias D. Davis too turned his B-17 back toward the North Sea. Fifteen minutes later, Vernon K. Cole's Fortress intercepted a rocket from a Ju-88, and became the first 306th plane to be shot down. It crashed in eastern Belgium, scattering its parachuting survivors in both Holland and Belgium. Robert McCallum's plane went down five minutes later, at 1:40, on the outskirts of Aachen, Germany. The firepower of these five planes had been lost even before the battle became severe. The remaining thirteen 306th bombers pulled together to close up the gaps in their formation as they approached Aachen, at the south end of the Ruhr valley. There was sporadic Flak near the cities, beginning with Antwerp, and later at Aachen and Coblenz, but the mission course had been plotted to avoid known Flak concentrations.

*   *   *

The crews of the twin-engined Messerschmitt Bf-110 Zerstörer of the Second Group of Zerstörergeschwader 76 (II./ZG 76) painted shark mouths on the noses of their aircraft (resembling those of the American Flying Tigers) and were known as the *Haifischgruppe* (Shark Group). This elite unit was stationed in October 1943 at Ansbach, fifty-five miles south of Schweinfurt. They scored very well indeed against the Flying Fortresses on Second Schweinfurt but, because of their more limited mobility, pilots of the twin-engined Bf-110s had little chance of surviving an encounter with the P-47 fighter escorts. For this reason they held back until the American air armada passed Aachen and the bombers' "Little Friends" had left for home.

One of the Zerstörer pilots was *Oberleutnant* (1st Lieutenant) Herbert Schob.[3] By 1943, Schob was already a Luftwaffe ace with a long and successful combat record, having registered more than ten aerial victories—or "kills." Schob had obtained his pilot's license on October 26, 1936. One of his first assignments was as a "volunteer" fighter pilot with the Condor Legion, Germany's contribution to General Franco's revolutionary forces in the Spanish Civil War. Originally commanded by General Hugo von Sperlle, in October 1938 the Legion was turned over to General Helmuth Volkman, then to Baron Wolfram von Richthofen. The conflict in Spain gave Göring's fledgling Luftwaffe opportunities to gain experience for its role, a few years later, as the spearhead for blitzkrieg in western and eastern Europe. Schob flew as an enlisted man with the Legion's 2nd squadron of fighter group Jagd 88, equipped with the new, but then unproven, Messerschmitt Bf-109.

In Spain, then-*Unteroffizier* (Staff Sergeant) Schob was stationed at a fighter base near the town of La Cenia, a few miles west of the Mediterranean coast. During the "Mediterranean Offensive" he and his fellow pilots flew fighter cover for bomber and Stuka dive-bombing sorties, and search-and-destroy missions against government Loyalist positions. They regularly met and shot down attacking American Curtiss Hawk and Russian I-16 Polikarpov Mosca (but called *Rata,* for "rat," by their opponents) fighters. The Soviets provided the latter planes, but they usually were flown by Spanish pilots. On October 13, 1938, Schob shot down a Curtiss fighter, one of the six aerial victories he claimed in Spain. His Messerschmitt Bf-109 carried the letters "NNWW" on the fuselage beside the cockpit, the abbreviation for a popular slogan he made his own, *Nur nicht weich werden* ("Just never be weak!"). It was a symbol he continued to use throughout the war.

The Condor Legion returned to Germany for a victory parade in Berlin in June 1939. Schob had little time to relax: three months later he was again in combat, and he claimed a victory flying a Zerstörer on September 1, 1939, the first day of the German invasion of Poland. In the Scandinavian campaign, now an *Oberfeldwebel* (Master Sergeant), Schob shot down a British Royal Navy "Skua" dive bomber at the Trondheim fjord in Norway in June 1940. He later served in the campaign in Greece, posing in Athens for a photograph, like many another tourist, at the Acropolis. The Balkan campaign over, he served with Zerstörergeschwader 26, flying on the Russian front, where he claimed his tenth aerial victory.

By the fall of 1943 he was back in Germany, flying a Messerschmitt Bf-110 with Zerstörergeschwader 76. Tall and slender when he obtained his pilot's license in 1936, photographs taken in 1943 and later show Captain Schob as a stocky, serious airman with a receding hairline. On July 9, 1944, he received the *Ritterkreuz*— the Knight's Cross to the Iron Cross—from Colonel-General Hans-Jürgen Stumpff, who, as commander of Luftflotte Reich, was responsible for German home defense.

*   *   *

According to his flight log, *Oberleutnant* Schob, with the remainder of his Zerstörer group, scrambled from the alert hut at Ansbach at 1:00 p.m. He and his radio operator scurried up a metal ladder into Zerstörer GL+NK, stepped across the wing root to the cockpit, settled into their seats, and adjusted their oxygen masks and throat microphones. The mechanics in their black overalls, the *schwartzen Männer* ("Men in black"), called *"Frei"* ("Start engines"), and Schob replied in kind as the twin engines roared to life and the instrument panel needles flickered back in response. The wheel chocks were pulled aside and, as he eased up on the throttle, the Zerstörer moved first sluggishly, then accelerated down the runway; its tail lifted slowly and the plane rose into the clear sky.

As the ground fell away, Schob banked the plane to the northwest. The radio operator tuned into the Reich fighter frequency (*Reichsjägerwelle*), which provided him with the coordinates for their rendezvous with the American bomber stream and a running commentary on aerial action over Germany. East of Aachen there were only scattered cirrus clouds above 25,000 feet, with excellent visibility for eight to twelve miles. Flying up the winding valley of the Main River, Schob climbed steadily toward the area east of Frankfurt.

By the time he was airborne the first elements of the American bomber stream were east of Antwerp and approaching the German border near Aachen. Streaking westward at 350 MPH, Schob passed high over the southern part of the Spessart—a hilly, wooded area of Germany closely resembling the Ozark Highland of southern Missouri—and the high range known as the Hahnenkamm ("Cock's Comb").

East of the Rhine, and north of Frankfurt, Schob's group spotted the B-17s at about 24,000 feet. The Germans began their attack about 2:00. Ten minutes later Schob registered a victory. Pulling up the nose of his Zerstörer, he launched his rockets, two at a time, into the bomber stream. He claimed a Flying Fortress at 2:10, somewhere east of Frankfurt, making it possible—despite the confusion that afternoon—that he was the pilot responsible for downing the *Wicked WAAC* or one of its sister ships. Schob filed the air victory confirmation (*Abschussbestätigung*) with the Luftwaffe High Command (OKL) later that day.

*   *   *

Herbert Kist, radio operator on another Messerschmitt Bf-110 (from the First Group of II./ZG 76, stationed in Wertheim am Main), recalls that his group assaulted the B-17s west of Schweinfurt. They attacked the bombers in *Staffel* formation—that is, about twelve planes abreast. The rockets were set to burst among the bomber formations. Since they fought so close to their station, they were able to make two, and sometimes three, attacks on the B-17s.

After a sortie they returned to base, where the armorers loaded the planes with more rockets and ammunition while other crewmen refueled the aircraft. Fliers did not like the rockets: they reduced their airspeed by as much as 40 to 110 kilometers per hour. The planes were also cumbersome in air combat because of their weight. The rockets were stripped from their planes in early 1944 because the weapon had not met the expectations placed on it. Crews were delighted.

*   *   *

This was Wood's first close encounter with enemy aircraft. On his previous five combat missions, for the most part, the weather and friendly fighter escorts had kept the German fighters well away from the *Wicked WAAC*, but October 14 was a deadly initiation into the fraternity of air combat. There were simply too many enemy aircraft to count. The Fortress shuddered with the recoil of .50-caliber machine guns, firing from all positions. Focke-Wulf 190s and Messerschmitt Bf-109s, blinking yellow on their wing edges, fired their machine cannons with explosive projectiles and their machine guns with armor-piercing ammunition.

One of the jobs of a B-17 navigator, besides keeping track of their position by heading and checkpoints, was to note in his log the time and place of Flak, fighter attacks, and enemy aircraft kills by the crew. Most such logs were sorely ignored or abandoned that afternoon as navigators manned the machine gun over their worktable to protect their aircraft.

From the time they entered German airspace the bomber stream was under attack by wave after wave of fighters, and the B-17s' machine guns were firing almost continuously, shaking the bomber with their vibrations. The smell of gunpowder would have been overpowering had the many bullet and 20-millimeter cannon holes in the skin of the aircraft not swept it away. In the nose of the plane and in the waist gunners' compartment, ejected .50-caliber shell casings lay ankle deep on the floor. The 500 rounds available for each gun were being expended at a frantic rate and, since those rounds comprised only one minute of firing time, many gunners would not have enough to last for the rest of the mission.

Save for the drone of the motors and their own machine-gun fire, the only sounds heard by the crew were those of shells striking the Fortress, as well as an intermittent shower of metal parts— fragments of other B-17s and fighters, shrapnel from Flak and rocket bursts, and machine-gun casings tumbling back from the bombers in front of them. Over the Rhine River, between

Andernach and Neuweid, Willard H. Lockyear's B-17, flying just behind the *Wicked WAAC*, was struck by rockets. It fell flaming to the ground near the town of Neuweid, with the loss of four of its crew.

Lockyear's B-17, flying at Bettinger's left, was the third 369th plane to be shot down. The loss of these three planes, together with the three B-17s that aborted earlier, stripped the 306th of sixty-six of its defensive .50-caliber machine guns. Each bomb group consisted of three squadrons—a high, lead, and low unit—that formed a staggered combat "box" flying in a precise formation, tightly spaced. The aircraft were stepped in the air both horizontally and vertically. The lead squadron was in front; the high squadron was to the right and slightly above and behind the lead; and the low squadron was to the left and slightly below and behind the lead (see the diagram on page 102). This complex arrangement provided mutual, massed protective fire for the group.

Cones of fire from the ten machine guns on each B-17 covered the sky for 1,000 yards in every direction. An incoming enemy fighter had to enter the cross-cutting fire of the machine guns, each of which provided maximum coverage for the individual aircraft and the group. When a B-17 aborted or was shot down, the remaining aircraft maneuvered to close up the gap. The box formation was difficult to maintain under the best of circumstances, for the slipstream of each plane created turbulence for those behind it, and each pilot was perpetually adjusting his controls to maintain the close intervals the formation demanded. In combat it was even more difficult, as the aircraft maneuvered to avoid collisions with one another and enemy aircraft, and to avoid being zeroed in on by enemy Flak batteries. There was a constant rearrangement of the Fortresses of the 306th as it bored deeper into Germany and suffered continuing losses.

During the mission, as was customary, the navigator kept the crew informed of their location, calling out towns to the bombardier so he'd be aware of their location in relation to the target. The last place Wood pointed out was Frankfurt: the 40th Combat

Wing passed about ten miles north of the city at 2:15, cruising at an altitude of 23,600 feet.

North and east of Frankfurt the 306th was dealt yet more damage in rapid succession. Four B-17s of the group were shot down within a little more than five minutes: those of John D. Jackson, Gustave S. Holmstrom, Douglas H. White, and George C. Bettinger. Jackson's Fortress was fatally damaged north of Frankfurt by Flak and fighters, and went down with the loss of four crewmen. A few moments later, near Hanau, gasoline began pouring from a large hole torn in the left wing of Holmstrom's *Picadilly Commando*. Asking his navigator for a heading to Switzerland, Holmstrom pulled out of formation and turned south. A German fighter followed them and continued its attack, and when the B-17 went into a dive the crew bailed out. Seven of them survived. A few moments later White's plane, attacked by a group of German fighters, also fell out of formation and was destroyed. It probably exploded, only one of the crew surviving. Bettinger's plane was lost about the same time.

The *Wicked WAAC* by now had already suffered damage, but the first crippling blow came with a rocket burst that destroyed much of the vertical stabilizer. Sergeant Gerking, firing his guns in the top turret, had a clear view of the stabilizer's destruction. The fuselage of the Fortress was also so badly damaged by 20-millimeter cannon shells from incoming fighters that, as Williams said, "You could have fallen out of some of the holes in the plane."

Next, the No. 3 engine, just to the right of the cockpit, was damaged in another attack and became a loud, screaming runaway, streaming a trail of smoke. As it accelerated to a speed of more than 2,500 RPM, it threatened to tear the engine from its wing mounting. Lieutenant Block cut off its fuel, but could not feather the engine, nor would it do so for Bettinger until he'd held the feather button down for several minutes. The propeller slowly turned its edges into the airstream and stopped rotating. With the loss of the engine their airspeed was reduced, and they began to drop back in formation. Stragglers were easy victims for even novice German fighter pilots, and Bettinger shoved the throttles of the remaining three engines to full acceleration in an effort to catch up with the rest of the group.

After the loss of the engine, Wood began working out a heading from the target area (which they still expected to bomb) to Switzerland, in the likely event a return to England was not possible. Dowden also told Bettinger to set the plane on auto-pilot, so if they could make it to the target he could bomb on his own. At the same time he opened the bomb bay doors, nearly sixty miles from the target. To this day he cannot explain why he did so.

Shortly after passing Frankfurt, Wood was struck in the stomach by shrapnel. He fell to the floor behind Dowden, and they exchanged a few words as Dowden crawled back to him, opened his chest parachute harness and his clothing. Opening the first-aid kit, he gave Wood a shot of morphine, poured a sulpha compound on the injury, and bandaged it with cotton and dressings. The bombardier replaced Wood's parachute harness and locked it in position. The only other thing he could do for the navigator now was pray. He turned back to his guns while Wood reattached the parachute to his harness. A moment later Wood tapped the bombardier on the back and touched his parachute, and Dowden helped him to the forward emergency exit door in the floor of their compartment, released it, and clamped Wood's hand around the parachute release ring. They said a few words to each other, then Dowden pushed him out of the escape hatch head first. Someone in the back of the plane radioed that his parachute opened.

The *Wicked WAAC*, responding to the increased acceleration, was beginning to catch up with the 306th planes ahead of her when a rocket damaged the left wing just outboard of the No. 1 engine and set the wing tip fuel tanks (the "Tokyo" tanks) and the engine on fire. Flames streamed out of the wing almost to the tail of the B-17. Bettinger immediately dived to the left and dropped out of formation to avoid blowing up other Fortresses if his aircraft exploded. He also applied fire extinguishers and put the plane in a steep dive, a strategy sometimes successful in efforts to blow out such fires. Schoolfield, the group leader, saw the *Wicked WAAC* drop out of formation and saw that it had a feathered engine, but he did not see the fire that followed the rocket burst on the left wing.

About this time, Lieutenant Dowden was struck in the left leg by 20-millimeter cannon shrapnel. There was no doubt it was broken, for his foot was twisted to one side. By now it was clear to him that the *Wicked WAAC* would not reach the target, so he tried to toggle the bombs from the bombsight. This didn't work, so he tried the manual salvo lever. It didn't work either, so he called Sergeant Gerking and told him to salvo the bombs using the release lever by the catwalk in the bomb bay. As Gerking did so, Dowden saw the lights go out on the instrument panel, showing the bombs had left the plane. Dowden then destroyed the Norden bombsight with several shots from a .45-caliber automatic, put on his parachute, and shoved himself through the emergency hatch.

*   *   *

Michelbach is a small community about twenty miles east of metropolitan Frankfurt am Main. It is one of many small towns sprinkled across the rolling hills of the western Spessart in Unterfranken (Lower Franconia), on the extreme northwestern margin of Bavaria. Before the war Michelbach had a population of about 1,500 people, and its main industry was a machine repair shop, and tobacco and wine production. The town lay on the north bank of the Kahl River, a small, west-flowing tributary of the Main.

The Spessart is one of the largest forested areas in Central Europe, but the region is sprinkled with a mosaic of open meadows, fields, and vineyards. The area is rich in history and legend— Charlemagne is reputed to have been born nearby on the Main River, and his soldiers are the first on record as having conquered the region. The red-tiled roofs of small picturesque villages, nestled in valleys along the many streams, punctuate the landscape like medieval preserves, some of the homes dating back to the twelfth century.

The forested hills between towns, mantled with beeches and oaks, are laced with footpaths, some of them bypassing the fortified ruins of Iron Age and Roman earthworks perched there. Other fortifications, like the castle in Alzenau, date to the Middle Ages. The quartzite-cored Hahnenkamm, south of Michelbach, is cloaked with oaks and, on this clear autumn day, sunlight filtered through the leafy kaleidoscope of greens and oranges, the trees casting soft shadows on the fern- and moss-covered forest floor. When the bomber stream began passing overhead in early afternoon, the morning mists had burned out of the valleys, and farmers were busy in their fields.

There was no industry in or near Michelbach to invite a direct air strike, and its inhabitants had little reason to fear the high-flying formations of Fortresses and Liberators. Enemy bombers until this time had been so rare over the homeland during the daylight hours that, during the Schweinfurt-Regensburg raid of August 17, many Germans actually waved at the massed formations passing over them, believing it was the Luftwaffe on parade.[4]

Cities in western Germany were, however, being repeatedly attacked by the Eighth Air Force, and in fact Frankfurt had been the target of massive round-the-clock air raids on October 4 and 5. Refugees had streamed out of the ruined residential areas of the city, and families throughout Unterfranken had taken them into their homes, raising the consciousness of the host families to the extent of devastation near industrial targets. By this time, night raids by the RAF also had destroyed large parts of many other industrial centers, military targets, and nearby residential areas, and destruction was beginning to assume alarming proportions for both military planners and the civilian population.

Then, too, there was Hamburg.[5] This major city in northern Germany, the second largest in the Third Reich, with a population of two million people, was almost obliterated by Operation GOMORRAH—a series of devastating raids by the RAF and the

Eighth Air Force in late July 1943. The city was leveled by a firestorm created by the thousands of incendiary bombs dropped into the wreckage left by high-explosive bombs. Flames reached a height of 15,000 feet over its melted ruins, and more than 45,000 people died during the bombardment or in the flames that consumed its debris. Six thousand acres of the metropolis were leveled, and three-quarters of a million people were made homeless in this national tragedy.

News of Hamburg's demolition and cremation spread to even the most remote parts of rural Germany, further fanning the hatred and terror that was building among the people for the Allied airmen they called *Luftgangsters* or *Terrorfliegers* responsible for such devastation. The presence in their homes and on their streets of the thousands of refugees left homeless by the raids made everyone feel uneasy. Hamburg also made Göring and the Luftwaffe, and the German High Command, acutely conscious of the threat posed by the Allied aerial campaign.

No contrails were visible that day, for the mission was being flown below 25,000 feet, and persistent contrails formed only above that altitude. On the ground, witnesses to the battle heard only the muted drone of the bomber fleet and the faint sounds of gun and cannon fire, and saw the B-17s only as flashes of light in the sky. The fighters attacking the bombers were too small to be seen.

At Kälberau, a small community just west of Michelbach, townspeople heard the distinct, distant drone of the First Air Division as it approached. People crowded the streets to watch and, as the sound grew, they saw the miniature forms of the *Pulk* ("herd") of Fortresses flying directly toward them, the individual bombers visible only as small dots against the sky. Otto Staab saw one of them catch fire directly overhead. It banked to the north and began a steep dive that carried it in the direction of Mömbris, parachutes streaming from it as it disappeared over the horizon. Normally, a wounded plane would be pounced on by German fighters and quickly dispatched, but the crew and ground witnesses remembered no further attacks after it dropped out of formation.

The massive damage to the *Wicked WAAC* was obvious, and the fact that it was on fire and the crew was abandoning it meant that further attacks weren't necessary. The German attackers therefore ignored it, keeping their attention on the rest of the B-17s as they continued on to the southeast, passing over the Ludwigsturm, an observation tower on the highest point of the Hahnenkamm.

The Luftwaffe air base at Langendiebach, near the town of the same name eight miles northwest of Michelbach, had been on alert since the bomber stream was first detected approaching the Continent. The alert at the base included mobilizing teams of men in trucks and touring cars to search for and capture airmen from downed planes. By 2:15 they could already see the thin trails of smoke from disabled B-17s north and east of the air base, and vehicles began moving toward points on the horizon where smoke trails and parachutes were visible. Most of the crew of the *Wicked WAAC* landed not far from one another and, since no other bomber was shot down within about fifteen miles of them, the men who landed near Michelbach can be identified as its crew members, though German accounts of their landing do not permit all of them to be individually identified.

CHAPTER EIGHT
BAILOUT OVER BAVARIA

Lieutenant Wood had already left the aircraft when Bettinger ordered the rest of the crew to bail out, but by this time the intercom was shot out and the message did not reach the crew members, nor could they call in. Neither was there a bell signaling a bail-out order; it too was disabled. Bettinger trimmed the plane so it was flying nearly level, set the auto-pilot, attached his parachute to his harness and dropped through the bomb bay. Block was badly hurt before he left the co-pilot's seat. A 20-millimeter cannon shell fragment had struck him in the shoulder, and he broke his collar bone as he dived out of the bomb bay.

Fortunately—especially considering his broken leg—Dowden's parachute dropped into a tree on a hillside beside the *Sportsplatz* south of Kälberau. He was picked up by soldiers and a group of civilians and taken into town and placed in an animal barn behind one of the houses. It was dark and he could only guess it was about 7:00 that evening when he was carried out of the barn and placed in a large stake-bed truck. Several newly captured airmen were in it, including Bettinger. Wood's body, his parachute wrapped around him, lay next to Dowden on the drive to Michelbach, where the dead navigator was taken from the vehicle and left on the sidewalk of the main street. The truck drove on to take the injured men to a hospital for medical attention.

Adalbert Simon, twelve years old, saw the *Wicked WAAC*

coming down, and walked through the woods with his father to the crash site on the Omersbach-Geiselbach road, about six kilometers from his home in Brücken. Meanwhile, a wounded airman walked to Simon's grandmother's restaurant in Brücken with the help of some local men, as it was the only place with a telephone. He was pale, with medium to dark wavy hair, handsome, and about 30 years old. He was wounded on one hand, and his back also was badly scraped. During his stay at the restaurant he was attended to by a Dr. Klug.

After two hours or so, a detachment from Langendiebach came for him. Before he was taken away, he gave the restaurant owner "a thin scarf" and an aluminum ring with a red stone in appreciation for her kindness. Donald Williams recalls that radioman Gordon Lewis was the only crewman on the *Wicked WAAC* to have a scarf made from a parachute, which may be the "thin scarf" he gave the woman.

Events in the air happened too quickly to recall clearly, but Williams believes that his gunfire from the left waist hit at least one enemy plane and left it smoking, but he has no idea whether he scored a kill. Early in the attack he was struck in the head by shrapnel and lost his oxygen mask, but Montana put another one on him and Williams continued firing. He was then shot through the left hand, and a piece of 20-millimeter cannon shrapnel hit him in the back—"it felt like about half of it!" he told this author. Williams tried to warn Mills in the belly turret that the plane was going down, and although he tried to help him out, the waist gunner was too badly wounded to do more than move himself to the waist window and bail out. One of his flight boots was torn off by the shock of the parachute opening. He lost a great deal of blood from his wounds, and his remaining boot was full of blood when he was picked up. As far as he could tell when he jumped, only Mills remained in the plane.

"I was getting some wonderful shots at incoming fighters," Mills said, "since there were plenty of targets to choose from. I think I shot down one plane that day, and possibly two of them. It seemed as though we were doing just fine, until I noticed something fly past me. Turning the turret, I saw it was one of the forward crew, whose parachute soon opened. A moment later another man parachuted as the forward crew continued to bail out. The interphone was shot out, so I didn't know the plane was being evacuated." When he tried to leave the turret, however, he discovered its hydraulic controls were out of commission. Moving quickly, he cranked the turret into the proper position to climb back into the fuselage, attached his parachute, and dropped out of the plane only moments before it crashed. He was the last man out of the B-17. He received only minor wounds in the fray.

*   *   *

The plane flew in a semi-circle before it crashed, and while the crew was parachuting. Erich Henkel of Geiselbach said that folks ran like rabbits as it circled over Omersbach and Geiselbach, since people had no idea where it would crash. On the outskirts of Krombach, Wilhelm Kampfmann watched the plane spiral down as the crew parachuted, and his future wife watched from a hill above Omersbach as the bombs salvoed from the *Wicked WAAC* exploded south of town. A piece of the aircraft fell from the plane and crashed to earth only a few yards from where she was standing.

October 14 was the birthday of one of the daughters of Mrs. Katharina Lorenz. Katharina and her two children were sitting around the coffee table in her sister's home in Omersbach to celebrate the event when they became aware of the noise of aerial combat. As they rushed into the yard they saw the bomber stream to the south, high above them. Minutes later they saw a B-17 approaching, trailing smoke, with parachutes resembling "white mushrooms" spilling open behind it. A moment later they heard the bombs jettisoned by Sergeant Gerking explode a few yards south of the village, and the shadow of the plane passed over them. It was so low they could feel the propeller backwash.

The explosion of the six 1,000-pound bombs as they plunged

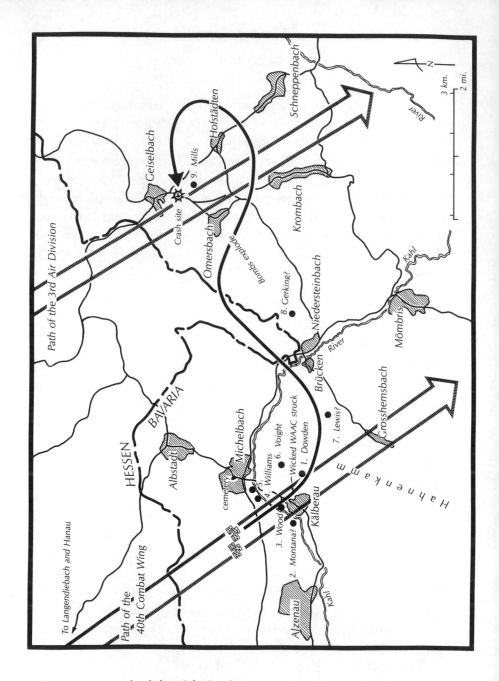

Approximate track of the 40th Combat Wing, First Air Division, on Second
Schweinfurt about 2:30 p.m., showing the crash site of the *Wicked WAAC*
and the parachute landing sites of nine of the crew. The map was compiled
from accounts and maps by several German eyewitnesses, each of which
varied somewhat in detail.

into a hillside on the outskirts of Omersbach shook the entire village. As Wilhelm Kampfmann wryly observed, "They left very large holes." Today only slight depressions remain where they cratered the side of the hill, for the farmer laboriously filled in the holes. Each of the craters took fifteen horse-drawn wagon loads of dirt to fill, but the earth has settled so that their points of impact are still visible.

After the bombs were jettisoned, the *Wicked WAAC* gained a little altitude, but soon continued its descent in a shallow curve. Unmanned now, it touched down in the broad, flat valley southeast of Geiselbach and skipped across an open field, rising briefly into the air several times and then crashing to the ground again. The ball turret was crushed and the mangled bomb bay doors were torn off as they dug into the earth, and tumbled along behind the plane. The propellers churned the soil in the field as they dug into the earth and were bent back flush with the engine cowlings.

The bomber headed directly toward the road on the low ridge between Omersbach and Geiselbach, a narrow, shaded lane lined by trees spaced about five yards apart. The mission ended abruptly when the *Wicked WAAC* smashed into the trees. The wings disintegrated as the plane rammed into their trunks, and when the fuel tanks ruptured, the remaining fifteen hundred gallons of gasoline aboard the aircraft exploded in a ball of white flame. Fingerlike plumes of flame erupted from the fireball and catapulted forward in gentle arcs, splashing to the ground. The burning fuselage and engines plunged through the trees as the bomber was torn apart, and debris catapulted in every direction. The fireball quickly turned crimson and expanded into a tower of black, roiling smoke that rose in a widening cone as it was blown to the southwest.

The four engines were torn from their mountings by the sudden impact and plunged across the road into an open field, tumbling to a stop just short of the Ungeheurer Grund—an area down the hillside named in medieval times and meaning, appropriately enough, "monster" or "dragon ground." The column of black smoke billowing up from the wreckage was visible for miles.

No one went near the plane until much later, for machine-gun bullets were exploding in the wreckage from the heat. Parts of the plane and machine guns were scattered for yards in every direction; ten charred steel helmets lay among them.

*   *   *

The explosion was witnessed by several farmers and their families who were nearby, working their fields that autumn afternoon. Heinrich Rienecker, a forty-four-year-old farmer who lived on Kirchstrasse in Geiselbach, was plowing in the field near the road using two teamed cows when the *Wicked WAAC* began its last descent. He and his eleven-year-old son watched the plane's descent. Transfixed by the event, or uncertain where to move to avoid it, he was only a few yards distant when the plane crashed and exploded. He died instantly of a brain concussion and other injuries when he was struck by flying debris and burning gasoline. Both cows also perished. His son, huddled in a shallow ditch along the road, escaped injury.

Young Thekla Peter and a French work prisoner, a *"Gastarbeiter"* ("guest worker"), had just arrived in the field from nearby Hofstädten with their cow-drawn cart, and were working only a few yards from Rienecker. Thekla was kneeling gathering potatoes, and the explosion blew her flat on her face on the ground. Burning gasoline splashed on her back and arms, and she rolled in the grass along the road to put out the flames, but they were not extinguished until one of the nearby farmers wrapped her in a blanket taken from the back of one of Rienecker's dead cows. In shock, she was taken home in her cart, and when she went to her room she saw the burns in the mirror; the skin was beginning to peel. "I looked," she said, "like a smoked ham." The pain came later.

The priest and Thekla's teacher soon came to visit, for she was not expected to live. The local doctor had no medication for her burns, but was able to give her morphine for the pain. He also prescribed schnapps for her heart. The family boiled oil, butter, and beeswax together to make a balm for the burns, and a nun came daily to change her bandages. She still carries terrible scars from the event and, as late as 1988, was yet undergoing operations to relieve complications resulting from her scars. Her left arm is three centimeters shorter than the other from one of these operations.

Witnesses report they later saw a twin-engined German Zerstörer briefly circling, high above the crash site. In all probability the pilot was confirming his destruction of the B-17. The plane, apparently a Messerschmitt Bf-110, then flew off to the northeast to rejoin the air battle that was now approaching Schweinfurt.

Not far from the crash site, eleven-year-old Erich Henkel and his school class were picking raspberry and strawberry leaves, from which tea was to be made for German soldiers. "There was," he said, "a terrible bang and we scattered in panic and fear." The youngsters watched in fascination, together with the crowd that quickly gathered, as the remains of the Fortress melted down from the heat of the fire. The tail was the only major part of the aircraft that remained identifiable after the wreckage cooled.

As witnesses to the disaster watched the flames lick into the sky, they saw the Third Air Division pass overhead, high over Omersbach, and directly over the pyre of the *Wicked WAAC*. The second wave of bombers was flying about six miles behind the First Air Division, parallel to its course, and four miles to the northeast. As it passed, .50-caliber machine-gun bullet casings ejected by the belly and tail turrets of other Fortresses in combat rained down across the landscape. People could see little puffs of dust rising in the dry fields where these and other pieces of debris landed from the air battle still raging overhead.

*   *   *

The crew of the *Wicked WAAC* landed at widely scattered locations, carried from their jumping points between the Hahnenkamm and Niedersteinbach by the wind blowing from the northeast. Most of them floated along the valley of the Kahl River and past the vineyards of the Weingut Höfler on the hills east of Michelbach, then over the town itself, to touch down in open country. Wood's parachute opened much higher than those of the others, since he was the first of the crew to leave the *Wicked WAAC*, and he left the plane when it was at an altitude of about 23,600 feet. Many crews were briefed to free fall when flying at high altitudes, but the novelty of the experience meant that few of them did so—for them it was their first jump.

Witnesses on the ground say Wood's parachute descended more quickly than those of the others, and that it was swinging wildly from side to side. He struck the ground very hard in a field a few yards from the south bank of the Kahl River, north of the railroad tracks midway between the towns of Michelbach and Kälberau.

Fourteen-year-old Alfred Sticker was near the church in Kälberau and, with Father Walter Zimowski, the assistant priest there, they watched the men parachute from the stricken bomber. From their vantage point on a hill overlooking the Kahl valley, they could clearly see the parachutes float toward them from the northeast. He later recalled the event in a letter in the Aschaffenburg *Main-Echo*:

"One of the parachutes was swinging back and forth in the air, and fell headfirst for part of the jump," Sticker wrote. Sticker and Father Zimowski began running down the hill and across the railroad tracks when the parachute touched down just east of the church. Before they reached the flier, a man carrying a gun ran to the prostrate airman and ordered him to his feet, shouting "Hands up!" A moment later, Sticker and Father Zimowski reached the flier and waved the man aside, saying, "Can't you see he can't stand?" The priest and Sticker unbuttoned his jacket, saw that his entire face was blue, and noticed his pulse was "very slow." Zimowski spoke with the flier in several different languages, but the airman showed no sign of life.

People from Kälberau were beginning to arrive, and soon a

large crowd of them surrounded the flier, but they were told, "Get back, move back." Some of them were hostile, but most were simply curious. Sticker and other witnesses said the flier's oxygen mask was not properly attached, but others believed his asphyxiation was because of strangulation by his parachute cords, some of which were wrapped around his neck. In panic, in confusion, or in shock, the airman had in all likelihood opened his parachute as he was falling facedown or while he was tumbling, and the lines had become entangled. The effect that the great altitude may have had on his wound is impossible to appraise, but it may have been a factor in his death—not to mention the consequences of the sudden jar of the parachute as it broke his fall. Then, too, if his oxygen mask was not properly attached, he may have rapidly lost consciousness in the thin air above 10,000 feet. If so, there is good reason to believe his death was painless. On the ground, despite attempts to resuscitate him, Sticker said, "the young American flier was beyond rescue." It is known that one of the crowd assembled that afternoon took a photograph of the young airman as he lay in the field.

*   *   *

In his haste the pilot, Lieutenant Bettinger, forgot to tighten the straps on his harness, so his chest parachute was not snugly attached. When he jumped, the Fortress was moving about 170 to 180 MPH, faster than the usual 155 MPH because of the speed built up during the dive to a lower altitude. When the chute opened, the shock fractured a vertebra in his lower back and he was knocked out. When he came to a few moments later, he saw the last man, Mills, drop free from the doomed ship.

Bettinger landed backwards in his parachute: on his heels, rump, and the back of his head. Immediately surrounded by a crowd, he was taken to a nearby small town where he sat on a stone curb, nursing the wounds in his lower legs. The villagers treated him as respectfully as he thought practical under the circumstances, although one woman who had recently lost a relative in the war slapped his face. Bettinger remained at the roadside until he was picked up by the Luftwaffe.

Another airman came down near the fire station in Kälberau. He is said to have fired a gun and resisted arrest: he was badly abused. This might have been Montana, as he was being beaten by a group of irate civilians when German soldiers arrived. Montana was wounded in the arm and back with shrapnel.

Two crewmen landed in a meadow on the southwest side of Michelbach, and were taken to the Gündling post office in Michelbach to await the military. One of them, Williams, was in much pain and had lost a great deal of blood, so his recollections for the next several hours are hazy. He nevertheless remembers sitting in a chair or sofa in front of a building along the street and being given help with his wounds, and being surprised that a nearby store had a Coca-Cola sign on it. Williams took a somewhat crushed D-bar, a chocolate bar supplied by the American Red Cross, from his coverall pocket and gave it to some young boys in the crowd that was growing around him. One of the boys, good-looking eight-year-old Edgar Handlbichler, was unafraid of Williams, and accepted the bar, for he had never tasted chocolate. A Nazi party official, however, took this treat from the boys and kept it himself, telling them, "One is not allowed to take something like this from an enemy." Eventually Williams was picked up by soldiers driving a large open touring car and taken to a hospital for treatment.

Another crewman landed on a steep slope in the forest on the west side of the Hahnenkamm. His foot was injured, so the man appears to have been Linden Voight, whose right foot had been blown off by shellfire in the *Wicked WAAC*. His troubles were not over, because, as Voight said, "I struck a tree when I landed and broke my right elbow and dislocated my right shoulder. Then I fell from the tree and broke my left foot."[1] He was found later, lying on the ground.

Arthur Weigand of Kälberau was one of the first people to

reach him, and gave him a Mollebusch pear that he had in his pocket. He then helped three men carry him down the hill sitting in his flier's jacket. Before reaching town the district magistrate drove toward them in his car. He got out and, as Wilhelm Kampfmann reported, "gave the American a strong boxing on his ears, and told him to get in the car. As they drove away, the flier waved to the men who'd carried him down to the road." When they arrived in Michelbach, they waited for soldiers to pick him up in front of Dr. Binder's house on the main street. "Suddenly," according to Kampfmann, "an official approached in his car, got out with his pistol at his side, hit the airman and ordered the forty to fifty people present to kill him. Men opposing this action were shouted down," but the event was resolved safely with the arrival of the Luftwaffe from Langendiebach.

A parachute also came down in the woods on the east side of the Hahnenkamm. The man was hurt and was arrested by some young men. They divided the captured material: the boys from Brücken took the prisoner into town, and the boys from Grosshembach kept the greater prize: the parachute. Parachutes were treasured possessions, for the white silk was ideal for making women's undergarments. If a parachutist was not captured soon after landing, his parachute would as often as not vanish into a farmer's haystack or hayloft, leaving searchers to speculate about how many airmen had landed, and where.

Gustav Wissel, chauffeur for a Wehrmacht general, was home on leave, and out hunting in the hills near his home in Niedersteinbach. He'd seen the burning B-17 pass low over the town, when suddenly one of the crew dropped directly in front of him in a clearing in the forest. The man took off his parachute, then tore a "mosquito" (symbol of the 369th Squadron) from his uniform and tried to hide it, for there was a general rule against wearing squadron insignia on missions. Wissel wanted to go to the crash site, and, with the downed American, began walking to Geiselbach. After hiking for about thirty minutes, however, a hostile crowd began to form around them, and some of the Germans would have killed the flier had Wissel not insisted, "This man is my prisoner."

Abandoning the trip to the crash site, they turned back and went to Niedersteinbach, where the airman sat on the side of the road until the military came to pick him up. The crowd remained hostile, and when Wissel tried to give him a glass of water it was knocked from his hand and splashed over the flier's face. A woman who had lost a relative in an air raid on Frankfurt spat on him and slapped his face. When the Luftwaffe arrived, the officer in charge gave the flier a cigarette—an act that let the crowd realize its behavior was unwarranted. The Nazi Bürgermeister of Niederstein-bach later told Wissel that his ration card would be taken away because he had "protected an enemy." When Wissel returned to duty and told his superior officer what had happened, he was given an additional two weeks of leave for having acted properly in his treatment of the flier. This man was probably Gerking, since he was the only man in the plane who was not wounded.

Elmer Mills, the last man to parachute, would have been killed had he jumped even a few seconds later, for he dropped out of the B-17 less than a mile from where it crashed, and he slammed into the ground only seconds after his parachute opened. Erich Henkel said, "He jumped when the plane was only about 150 meters above the ground." He was badly beaten by the crowd that surrounded him, after which he was taken to the fire or police station in Scholl-krippen. He'd hurt his foot and could not walk very well, and his face was so battered and swollen from his beating that when Donald Williams saw Mills a few hours later he scarcely recognized him.

*   *   *

B-17 crews were landing at widely separated places across central Germany. Some of the men were taken prisoner without incident; some were abused by civilians, as Montana and Mills had been; and still others fared even worse at the hands of the Gestapo.

A Fortress returning from Schweinfurt on only two engines

made a forced landing in northern Bavaria, between the towns of Rengersbrunn and Ruppertshütten, twenty-four miles due east of the crash site of the *Wicked WAAC*. A nurse from Ruppertshütten saw the plane land and went immediately to it, but when she arrived the crew was gone, although she found blood spattered in the fuselage. She went home to get first-aid supplies and returned to the site with a police lieutenant. By that time the Gestapo had taken four of the crew into custody; they shot the men a few minutes later. The airmen were buried in the cemetery at Ruppertshütten. When United States troops entered the town on April 3, 1945, they were told of the execution and, in the summer of 1946 when an American military court in Dachau reviewed the murder of the airmen, the leader of the execution squad was sentenced to death and hanged.[2]

* * *

Two hours after the *Wicked WAAC* crashed and exploded, a twin-engined German plane appeared. It dived down and briefly circled the black pillar of smoke that marked the B-17's ruins, then disappeared. The plane, painted black on its underside, was in all probability a Ju-88 from the night-fighter group (*Nachtjagdgeschwader*) at Langendiebach making a survey of Eighth Air Force losses on Black Thursday. Its pilot, or another Luftwaffe pilot, came to Geiselbach later that afternoon to inspect the wreckage, and visited the Rienecker family.

Soldiers came later that day and cordoned off the wreckage and placed a guard on it to prevent pilfering. A few days later, local farmers helped collect the debris, which was carried to the *Sportsplatz* in Geiselbach. The older school children of the town were assigned to pick up the .50-caliber ammunition that was scattered around the crash site by the exploding fuel tanks. It often took as many as four days to clean up the remains of a heavy bomber, but since so much of the *Wicked WAAC* had been destroyed by the fire, the job was finished in less time. The debris from the Fortress was carried away by trucks from the air base at Langendiebach to a railroad siding in Hanau. The trucks made several trips, because it normally required three railroad cars to transport the wreckage of a heavy bomber. The final destination of the B-17 was a salvage yard.

Each Allied aircraft downed in German-held territory was thoroughly investigated by salvage details from the Berge Bataillone, a unit under the operational control of the Luftwaffe. Each B-17 and B-24 provided more than 15 tons of potentially useful metal and parts and, as the air war over Europe accelerated, this salvage became an increasingly important source of raw material. Although the charred remains of the *Wicked WAAC* were suitable only for scrap, usable equipment on better-preserved bombers was reclaimed and supplied to Luftwaffe units that operated captured or rebuilt Allied warplanes as part of their continuing investigation of enemy weapons. Allied bombers and fighters that were recovered nearly intact were repaired and later flown by the special Kampf-geschwader 200 of the Luftwaffe, training German pilots in how best to attack the Allied aircraft.

Most downed planes were too badly damaged to be repaired, and the aluminum-alloy scrap from them was simply cut into pieces, melted down, and recycled. The ingots were shipped to German aircraft factories so, by this means, B-17s and other Allied aircraft were transformed into Messerschmitts and other fighters that eventually took to the air against the Allied air armadas.

Throughout 1943 and early 1944 the scrap from all aircraft shot down over Germany and the occupied countries was taken either to a salvage yard at Nanterre-Paris, France, or to one at Utrecht, in The Netherlands. As the aerial offensive against the Reich mounted, other yards were established in Germany itself. The returns from this cannibalistic operation were impressive: in November of 1943 alone, the smelting operation at Utrecht processed over 154 tons of aluminum.[3] Utrecht is only 225 miles north of Michelbach, so the scrap yard there is probably the one where the last recognizable parts of the *Wicked WAAC* were reduced to ingots to become part of the arsenal of the Luftwaffe.

*   *   *

At Thurleigh the beds of the missing crewmen were stripped, and
their personal belongings were quickly removed from the barracks.
Replacements were hurriedly brought in to fill the empty bunks.
On November 22, 1943, the belongings of Lieutenant Wood were
received by the Quartermaster Corps' Advanced Air Depot No. 2,
APO 635, somewhere in England, for shipment to the United
States. Although it was general practice for the group commander
to send the family a personal letter on the death of one of his men,
or when they were missing in action, the simultaneous loss of one
hundred men from the group strained this policy: the family heard
nothing directly from Station 111.

*   *   *

The *Wicked WAAC*, B-17 Flying Fortress Serial Number 42-30199,
had been delivered new to the 306th Bomb Group on August 31,
1943. When it crashed on October 14 it had seen only one and a
half months of service. The Fortresses lost in Second Schweinfurt
were replaced by late October, and another B-17 took the place of
Bettinger's aircraft: B-17 Serial No. 42-31078 assumed the role of
the *Wicked WAAC* in the 369th Bomb Squadron, and an "R" was
painted on its tail.[4] This plane remained in service for only about
a month, for on December 11, piloted by John P. Noack, it was
lost in a raid on Emden, Germany. Noack had been the pilot of
one of the five planes that bombed Schweinfurt and returned to
Thurleigh two months earlier. His luck had run out: he became a
prisoner of war.

*   *   *

Of the ten men who took off in the *Wicked WAAC* on October 14,
1943, only the engineer, Gerking, escaped without a scratch. Everyone else was wounded, but only the navigator did not survive
the day.

Dowden was hospitalized for the entire time he was in Germany, spending most of his time at Oflag (officer's camp) 9A/H, until he was repatriated in 1945. Everyone on the surviving crew was first sent to Dulag (transient camp) Luft, the Luftwaffe reception camp for Allied air force prisoners of war. Dulag Luft was a scattered complex of buildings between Frankfurt and Oberursel, a small town northwest of the city. There were interrogation and solitary confinement cells at Oberursel. All incoming fliers spent a week to thirty days here in what was, in effect, a short-term holding camp for all captured non-Soviet airmen while they were being interrogated, and before they were sent on to permanent prisoner of war camps. Because so many incoming fliers were in need of medical attention, Hohemark Hospital, about a mile west of the interrogation center, was requisitioned for their treatment.

At Oberursel the men were photographed, fingerprinted, and placed in solitary confinement before being interrogated. Bettinger was in solitary for a week, then was sent to a prison hospital at Obermassfeld, where his leg wounds were treated. His final destination was Stalag Luft III at Sagan, where he and Abraham Block were imprisoned in South Camp.

German doctors operated on Block and on Williams in the same room. But, as Williams expressed it, they used no ether: "They didn't even use a blackjack." From his stretcher Williams could hear them cutting on Block, but he never heard the co-pilot utter a sound during the ordeal.

After his release from Obermassfeld, Williams was sent to Stalag XVII-B, near Krems, Austria. He was joined by Gerking, Lewis, Mills, Montana, and, until his repatriation in 1944, by Voight. Williams, Montana, and several other men were taken by train to Krems, then by truck to Stalag XVII-B. During the ride, Voight complained that his missing foot was cold, so Williams put his remaining flight boot over the stump, and Voight told him, "Thanks. It's warmer now." Mills and Montana were bunkmates. Mills said he escaped from camp three times, once with Thomas

McMahon, but was recaptured each time. Stalag XVII-B was liberated by General George S. Patton's Third Army in 1945. Williams was left with a short left leg from his wounds, and he picked "scrap iron" out of his head for years after the war.

Ralph Ellsworth, waist gunner on Holmstrom's B-17, was sent to the same hospital as Voight, since he'd lost several fingers in the attack. "Voight," he told me, "had a rough time of it. They put him to sleep in the hospital just before they did me. They used ether. After the operations they put us on stretchers and put us on a train and took us to another hospital. Gerking came to me as we were leaving and thought my whole right leg was gone because the leg on my flying suit was torn to shreds. Gerking didn't get a scratch.

"When Voight's foot was removed," Ellsworth continued, "they didn't cut the bone back and pull the muscle over the end for a pad, but cut it straight across, just above the ankle. They simply pulled the skin down to grow over the end. He suffered a great deal, and one day when a British doctor (who'd been captured at Dunkirk) came by, Voight called him over to ask for something to kill the pain. After the doctor left, an orderly arrived with two aspirins. The next time he saw the doctor he said, 'Two aspirins aren't very much to give me for what I'm going through.' The doctor replied that in *their* army officers were given more respect than in *his* army. Voight's response was that 'He may be a good officer, but as a doctor he isn't worth a good God damn.' The doctor later cut the bone back and fixed the leg right, and gave him something that did help the pain."

Voight and Dowden were sent home on prisoner exchanges in 1944 and 1945. They had been examined by Swiss doctors and, because neither of them was fit for duty, they were exchanged for injured German prisoners of war. Dowden's experience as a German prisoner is chronicled in his book, *One and One Half Missions,*[5] that describes his long ordeal in German hospitals at Obermassfeld, Meiningen, and Annaberg. His leg, threatened with amputation, was saved by an Australian doctor and prisoner at Obermassfeld, but a long recuperation followed before he was released, returning to the United States on the Swedish cruise ship *Gripsholm.*

*   *   *

Herbert Schob was one of the rare German pilots to fight throughout World War II and survive, a member of the fortunate fraternity who, like Adolf Galland and some others, was among "the first and the last" to fight in the air. The attrition among fighter pilots in the Luftwaffe was frightening indeed, particularly in the last phases of the war.

In June 1943, Major Hajo Herrmann, famed for having initiated night fighting for the Luftwaffe, was ordered by Göring to form a new wing of "Wild Boar" fighters. The unit, Jagdgeschwader 300, better known as the *Rammjäger* ("Ram Fighters"), flew Focke-Wulf 190s from a base near Salzburg. At the twilight of the war—by March 1945—the lack of fuel and ammunition severely curtailed the aggressive activities of the *Rammjäger.* Schob's final transfer was to this unit, and he ended his military service with this group, flying what few missions were possible with their reduced supplies.

JG/300 was dissolved unceremoniously when the news arrived that American ground forces were advancing toward them along the autobahn. The men began melting into the countryside, slowly making their way home. Schob was by this time a captain (*Hauptmann*), with 500 combat missions, and credited with twenty-eight air victories: six in Spain, and including ten four-engined Allied bombers. He died in Frankfurt in April 1981.

CHAPTER NINE

A FUNERAL IN GERMANY

Andreas Noll had been the Bürgermeister of Michelbach for thirty-one years—since 1912. Born in Offenbach, a few miles southeast of Frankfurt, before the turn of the century, he'd been too old to serve in the military in World War I. Sometime before the war he'd come to Michelbach and opened a bakery, and became the Bürgermeister a little later. Although it was customary for a Bürgermeister to be a member of the Nazi Party during the Third Reich, Noll remained in office throughout World War II despite his lack of membership. Because of his long term in office, Noll carried out his official duties pretty much as he liked. In many cases he disregarded instructions given, for example, by the municipal council.[1]

Because there was no morgue in Michelbach at the time, Lieutenant Wood's body was laid out in the fire equipment station on Schlosstrasse. Noll did not know what to do with the body, so he contacted the Luftwaffe station at Langendiebach and asked them to evacuate the navigator's body. He was told the remains should be taken care of by local authorities, although the death certificate should be made out by a military surgeon.

Dr. Ludwig Reichert, the doctor from Alzenau, had first been asked to conduct an examination of the flier's body, but he was later told that the examination would be made by military medical personnel. From an unofficial private medical interest, however, he examined the body the day after the raid. As far as he could remember, he found no shot wounds or fractures, but he was told that parachute shroud lines had been found wrapped around the airman's throat. The parachute was no longer with the body, having been taken by the Luftwaffe detachment that recovered Wood. Reichert believed the cause of the American's death was due either to acute heart failure following a jump from great altitude without an oxygen mask, or strangulation by the cords. On January 17, 1946 (when he filed a report on the incident with the United States Office of Military Government at Alzenau), however, he could recall finding no trace of suffocation, although he was still of the opinion that the cause of death was strangulation by the parachute shroud lines.

The day after Second Schweinfurt, on Friday, a Medical Corps Captain (*Stabsarzt*) from the Luftwaffe appeared at the town's city hall to interview Bürgermeister Noll. He and Noll walked across the street to the firehouse, where the officer examined the body and removed Wood's identification tags. He told Noll that one tag would be sent to German authorities and the other to the International Red Cross—although eleven weeks would pass before, on December 31, 1943, the War Department in Washington, DC, received notification of Wood's death.

The *Stabsarzt* also gave Noll a permit to bury the body of the enemy airman. When Noll asked him how this was to be done, he was told, *"Das ist Ihre Sache!"* ("That's your business"). Having no other options, Noll acted as he felt was proper in the circumstances. He ordered a local carpenter, Valentin Wegstein, to build a wood coffin and make a wood cross for the airman. According to an entry in Wegstein's workshop book, he made the coffin on Saturday, October 16. The inscription on the cross was prepared by Karl Norgang, a painter, who found the order to paint the cross in his workshop with a slip of paper bearing the inscription *Grabstätte* [Grave site] *des Elbert C. Wood, 14 Oktober 1943*.

Although he had never been a soldier, Noll felt that a military casualty should be buried with military honor, so he ordered all

German soldiers who were home on furlough in Michelbach to attend the funeral. Seven members of the Wehrmacht appeared in uniform on Sunday, October 17. One of the soldiers, Peter Hofmann, said Noll "organized the funeral in the courtyard of the castle" (the Schlösschen, an impressive structure in downtown Michelbach with corner towers) which adjoined the firehouse where Lieutenant Wood's body had lain. Two non-commissioned officers and five privates comprised the military honor guard. They included Ferdinand Pfeifer; Sergeant Peter Hofmann, an ambulance attendant; and Karl Hee, who'd been discharged from the Wehrmacht because of a severe wound. Other witnesses included Sebastian Jung, the Hitler Youth leader in Michelbach; a representative of the Wehrmacht from the Alzenau Military Hospital; and several civilians and children.

The group carried the coffin four blocks north up the cobblestone street, past the Michelbach city hall and the Catholic church, to the small Catholic cemetery on the north side of the town. It was surrounded by a low stone wall, beyond which, to the north, were the low rolling hills that mark the northern boundary of Bavaria. To the south were the red-roofed homes and businesses of wartime Michelbach. The grave had been dug before the small procession arrived: a previous occupant of the plot in which Wood was to be buried had been exhumed and his body moved.

Father Franz Ruf, the Catholic priest in Michelbach, is also said to have conducted a funeral for Wood—"according to the customs of the Michelbach church community and Roman Catholic rites." He recalled in 1988 that he "probably also conducted a mass afterward for the salvation of the deceased" in the Michelbach church.

Bürgermeister Noll and Karl Hermann, the cemetery caretaker, performed the burial at the cemetery, which Noll said had a "serious and official" character. Noll made a little speech in which, he said, he pointed out that the airman had fought and died for his country and that the German soldiers were present in his honor. He also commented that the possibility existed for the

German soldiers present at the funeral to be "confronted with the same fate." The soldiers saluted while the coffin was covered with earth.

The plot in which Lieutenant Wood was laid to rest was near the wall at the back of the cemetery, next to Edmund Kerker, the father of the wife of Peter Hofmann, one of the soldiers who attended the funeral. The wooden cross was fastened to a stone base, and the grave planted with flowers. A few days after the funeral a Luftwaffe sergeant arrived in Michelbach and took the certificate of burial from Noll. On Noll's order, the grave was kept in good condition. In February 1945, a German soldier was buried between Lieutenant Wood and the stone wall.

From the beginning of the 19th century it has been the obligation of an enemy state to provide respectable burials for prisoners of war. Furthermore, Article 4 of the Geneva Convention of July 27, 1929 (often called the "Prisoners of War Code," and to which Germany was a signatory), clearly specifies that belligerents shall collect and "forward to each other all objects of personal use found on the field of battle or on the dead, especially one-half of their identity plaque, the other half remaining attached to the body. They shall see that a careful examination, if possible, medical, is made of the bodies of the dead prior to their interment or cremation, with a view to verifying their identity, and in order to be able to furnish a report thereon. They shall further see that they are honorably buried and that the graves are treated with respect and may always be found again." Lieutenant Wood's treatment was fully in accord with the Convention except that both of his "dog tags" were removed.

Bürgermeister Noll jeopardized himself by his handling of Lieutenant Wood's funeral, for local Nazis believed he'd been "too considerate" of an enemy of the Reich. According to Edgar Handlbichler, military honors for bomber crewmen were forbidden by a regulation issued by Hitler, in violation of the spirit, at least, of the Geneva Convention of 1929. The grave was, however, well tended by local citizens. Peter Hofmann's wife, Elisabeth, often decorated the grave of the "handsome young American" when she visited the adjoining one of her father.

* * *

By March 1945 Allied armies had stormed across the Rhine and into western Germany, and American troops stood on the west bank of the Main River, ready to advance on the heart of the Reich. The Main was crossed on the night of the 22nd by General George S. Patton's Third Army, and by the 25th his troops stabilized their bridgehead across the river near Hanau. There were desperate efforts by the Germans to stem the breakthrough, but on March 25 their efforts were further thwarted when the bridges over the Main at Aschaffenburg were captured intact by General Alexander M. Patch's Seventh Army, whose troops, on the 28th, successfully crossed the river to establish another bridgehead.

Aschaffenburg was especially heavily defended in response to demands by local Nazi leaders, and news correspondents on the scene were quick to name its defenses the "Little Siegfried Line." Heavy artillery and attacks by fighter bombers were not enough to drive the German defenders out of the city. German officers who suggested surrender were hanged in the streets, and civilians joined the soldiers in resisting the American advance, some of them even throwing hand grenades from their homes. Bitter house-to-house fighting was expected to continue and, to avoid this costly undertaking, American commanders called for an aerial bombardment of the city. Much of the ancient town was reduced to rubble, including the famous castle, Schloss Johannisburg, a 17th-century landmark. Aschaffenburg's commander, Major von Lambert, surrendered the city only after most of it was reduced to rubble.[2]

With the fall of Aschaffenburg, called "Cassino on the Main" during the attack, General Patch's Seventh Army began pushing east into the Spessart. The soldiers of Charlemagne had been the first troops in historic times to conquer the Spessart, an event now to be rapidly repeated. On Patch's left flank, American troops quickly captured Alzenau and then directed their attention toward Michelbach and the upper Kahl River area and, further up the Main River, toward Schweinfurt. The 121st Squadron of the 106th Cavalry Group was ordered to take Kälberau and Michelbach, and their forces gathered in the forest east of Alzenau for the assault. On the morning of March 30, Good Friday, they began their drive up the valley toward their objectives. A description of the capture of the Kahl valley is told in detail in Alois Stadtmüller's 1982 *Maingebeit und Spessart im Zweiten Weltkrieg* (The Districts of Main and Spessart in World War II).

The upper Kahl valley had, until this time, endured very little direct war damage. An attack by the RAF on the night of April 11, 1943, scattered incendiary bombs near Alzenau and in the forests around Michelbach, but little property damage was done. Later raids led to several severe forest fires. In Michelbach, dugout shelters had been prepared both north and south of the town in the event of more severe incidents. On this Good Friday, however, the quiet lives of the residents of Michelbach changed. The townspeople were already under great hardship: the community was cut off from all newspaper and mail delivery, for neither cars nor trains were moving in or out of town, and enemy forces were advancing on them. Most of the town's citizens fled their homes and sought shelter in the forests north and east of Michelbach when a company of Kampfgruppe 388 moved into town and began to set up bunkers and machine-gun emplacements.

Kälberau also was fortified. Flak guns were dug in at the brick factory west of town. Their crews were all *Flakhilfers* less than sixteen years old, but these schoolboys were well armed with carbines and Panzerfaust (shoulder-fired anti-tank rockets). In the early afternoon of the 29th, American reconnaissance vehicles appeared east of town, and in the evening they appeared again in pursuit of some German soldiers. One American armored car approached too closely, and was destroyed by a Panzerfaust. Kälberau was attacked the next morning and, after a bitter contest, fell about noon.

The same morning, about 10:30, Michelbach was bombarded by 75-millimeter assault guns of the 121st Squadron of the 106th Cavalry Group. The railroad station and yards were devastated, and nearby houses were damaged. "When the barrage lifted the men were loaded on armored cars and halftracks and moved toward the town. A short distance from the first houses the men dismounted and followed the armored cars"[3] as they rolled into town, firing round after round into the houses and forcing the German infantry into the open, where the cavalry troops attacked them. A German machine gun at the crossroad in the south part of town was assaulted and taken after most of its crew were killed or wounded. Kampfgruppe 388 infantrymen, however, continued to fight under heavy fire in some of the damaged buildings until the town was surrendered, and the survivors then retreated, fighting, to positions east of town.

The battle for Michelbach lasted until about 1:00 p.m. After the street fighting ended, cavalrymen made a house-to-house search for German soldiers, abruptly beating in doors if they found them locked. When the few remaining civilians in town heard the conflict move off to the east they slowly came out of their cellars to see many of their homes in ruins, and a small group of neighbors silently watched the barn of Karl Huth burn to the ground. Three Americans were killed and three others were wounded during the conflict; the Germans lost many dead and wounded, and 177 prisoners were taken.[4] The 106th Cavalry troops continued up the Kahl valley, and the sound of fighting soon passed beyond earshot. Two days later, on Easter Sunday, Geiselbach surrendered.

Schweinfurt itself fell on April 11, 1945, to the 42nd Infantry Division (the famous "Rainbow Division") and the 12th Armored Division, units of General Patch's Seventh Army. Its surrender came after three raids on the now-devastated city by Martin B-26 Marauder twin-engined bombers. These attacks mangled the concentrations of German troops and armor in the city, following which an assault on Schweinfurt crushed final resistance. Four days after its surrender, a special Order of the Day was issued at

Headquarters, U.S. Strategic Air Forces in Europe: it formally announced that the strategic air war against the Third Reich was over, and that from that day forward Eighth Air Force bombers would be used in tactical operations in support of ground troops. It had been concluded that the long, costly campaign to destroy the industrial might of Germany was at last over.

Meanwhile, Schweinfurt had been the target for no less than sixteen American air attacks (and two British), during which 6,500 tons of bombs had been dropped since First Schweinfurt on August 17, 1943. The 42nd Infantry quickly lowered the red, white, and black Nazi swastika flag over the Kugelfischer factory, and the divisional commander turned it over to General Carl A. Spaatz, Commanding General, U.S. Strategic Air Forces in Europe. Spaatz, in turn, later forwarded it to the 305th Bomb Group, since this unit had suffered the heaviest losses during the long Schweinfurt campaign—nineteen bombers.[5] The 305th Bomb Group lost thirteen Fortresses on Second Schweinfurt, three more bombers than the 306th Bomb Group sacrificed that day.

Shortly after the surrender of the Kahl valley, American officers arrived in Alzenau to establish a local headquarters of the Office of Military Government. Well before the capitulation of Germany, Supreme Allied Headquarters in Europe established an automatic arrest policy for a wide category of Nazis, ranging from the top officials in Berlin down to mayors, police chiefs, and local leaders of the Hitler Youth. Many Nazis in western Germany fled their homes to escape arrest and, because *Landkreis Alzenau* was a rugged, out-of-the-way region of the homeland, noted for its isolation and sparse population, it was a favored refuge for them. Most of them were, however, not hard to find. "Nearly all suspects, once they were identified, could be brought in by postcards telling them to report to the detachment office at a specified time."[6]

In 1945, Andreas Noll was dismissed from his post as Bürgermeister by the United States Office of Military Government in Alzenau. He had been seen in a photograph together with some uniformed local Nazi Party officials, and so he was considered by the Americans to be politically unreliable. He had also been as high-handed with officials of the new United States military government as he earlier had been with his own. When German soldiers who illegally returned home from United States Army prisons were captured, they were tried and ordered to return to prison camps. When military representatives were late in arriving to escort the men in his jurisdiction back to prison, however, Noll sent the men home.

For these reasons Noll's long reign as Bürgermeister of Michelbach ended abruptly, but he is still remembered by residents as having remained in that position longer than any other municipal office holder in the area. He should also be remembered as a humane official who went out of his way to bury an American airman with dignity and honor, at a time when this was not a popular or even a safe course of action.

CHAPTER TEN

THE AMERICAN GRAVES
REGISTRATION COMMAND

In 1941, recognizing that America was facing potential overseas conflict, the United States Army initiated several moves to anticipate the casualties that inevitably would follow. The first move was to reestablish the Graves Registration Service, a unit that had been discontinued after World War I. The wartime activities of that service (1942–45) and those of the postwar American Graves Registration Command (1945–51)[1] were to be responsible for the location, identification, and interment of the remains of American military personnel who fell in World War II.

For nearly a century, Americans had been committed to the recovery, identification, and proper burial of the war dead, but only with the experience gained through involvement in several conflicts was it possible to accomplish in practice what had been supported in theory.

Special treatment, and ceremonies that honor or attempt to immortalize the warrior dead, have been customary for many societies over the millennia. Edward Steere, in *The Graves Registration Service in World War II*, for example, noted the similarity of sentiment and expression between the funeral oration of Pericles and Lincoln's Gettysburg Address. However, as he goes on to say, "It is a melancholy fact that only within the past hundred years has

161

any government been willing or able to assume the obligation of identifying and burying in registered graves the remains of all who gave up their lives in war."

Statistics for the treatment of American war dead begin with the Mexican War of 1846–47. In that conflict Congress created the innovative precedent of establishing military cemeteries abroad, although burial practices were abysmally poor: only ten percent of the war dead were identified.

Sentiment during the Civil War to honor the remains of those who gave their lives in defense of the republic led to a dramatic change in how war dead were treated. Within two months of the first major battle, at Bull Run, the War Department supplied forms to all hospitals so they might accurately record mortuary information for combatants who died, and directed that materials be provided for headboards to be placed over their graves. This led to a significant increase in the rate of identification, for Union soldiers at least. The vast numbers of dead, the lack of adequate cemeteries, and a general lack of planning nevertheless overwhelmed the system. The archaic practice of assigning burial details from front-line troops at the site of the battle was continued by both sides.

In 1862 Congress authorized the president to purchase land for cemeteries to be used for soldiers who died in the service of their country. Many of the burial sites for major battles were soon transformed into national cemeteries. Among the many such cemeteries founded by the War Department was the one at Gettysburg, as well as the most famous one, on Robert E. Lee's farm at Arlington, Virginia. A few months after the war's end, the practice also began of exhuming the remains of the fallen from scattered sites and concentrating them in these cemeteries.

The identification rate of Civil War dead varied. One hundred percent of those who died at Fort Stephens were identified, but other battlegrounds were neglected for up to four years, with a correspondingly miserable percentage of identified dead. Only fifty-eight percent of the Union war dead eventually were identified; the rate overall for both sides, however, was only forty-two percent of the victims of that conflict.

The next major developments in American burial policy resulted from the Spanish–American War, when the basic organization of modern graves registration in the U.S. armed forces was established. Military graves in Cuba were first marked, then the remains were disinterred and, casketed, were returned to the United States. The use of an aluminum identity disk (the first modern "dog tag") was advocated. The results: a new high of 86.4 percent of the dead were identified. Consequently, with the outbreak of World War I, Steere reports, "the way was paved for the establishment of specialized theater units for care of the dead."

The success in recovering and identifying World War I fatalities may be attributed to the establishment in 1917 of the Graves Registration Service (GRS) in the United States Army Quartermaster Corps. This organization was charged with collecting and identifying bodies, marking battlefield graves, keeping accurate mortuary records, and maintaining temporary burials and semi-permanent military cemeteries in Europe. Speed in registering war graves was critical, for experience gained from previous wars showed that the number of unknowns is directly proportional to the time lag between original burial and registration of the graves. World War I graves registration units followed closely on the heels of combat troops, thereby ultimately achieving a 96.5 percent identification rate for the more than 79,000 American war dead. Success did not come easily. The dangers and difficulties of service on World War I battlefields can hardly be exaggerated, especially when graves registration was taking place on active battlefronts that moved back and forth over collection and cemetery areas.

The unprecedented success of the World War I mortuary program confirmed that a special service was needed to perform the task of graves registration if the dead were to be recovered quickly, thereby maximizing identification. Consequently, a Graves Registration Service (GRS), modeled after the World War I organization, was established following the December 1941 bombing of Pearl Harbor at the onset of American entry into World War II. Recovery techniques followed *Technical Manual 10-630*, which was published four months earlier. Field units eventually were placed in all overseas theaters, but in World War II the GRS was most active in the European Theater, where more than two-thirds of the nearly 400,000 American combat fatalities occurred.

Like their World War I prototypes, World War II GRS units were charged with coordinating the collection, identification, and burial of the dead, but for reasons of efficiency several changes in procedure were made. For example, in contrast to the World War I practice, World War II fatalities were not buried in cemeteries at the battle sites. Instead, remains were evacuated first to battalion and then to division collecting points by teams detailed from combat units. At the collecting point every effort was made to establish the identity of the deceased by consulting members of their own units. This accomplished, the bodies were transferred to one of the temporary interment sites in Europe.

There were two advantages to this system.[2] First, the practice of identifying as many casualties as possible at the collecting point resulted in a reduction in the percentage of unknown bodies delivered to cemeteries. This procedure also allowed for concentrating burials in only a few cemeteries. At the close of hostilities in Europe 117,000 United States casualties were interred in only fifty-four cemeteries, whereas by the end of World War I, 75,000 casualties had been placed in 2,240 scattered burial areas. The World War II burial program was the largest of its kind ever attempted by any nation in history.

*   *   *

With the end of hostilities in Europe, the GRS of the Quartermaster Corps was replaced by the self-contained American Graves Registration Command (AGRC). This postwar organization, established July 1, 1945, took over the responsibilities of the wartime

Graves Registration Service, but with the cessation of combat, field units no longer collected and removed bodies from the battlefield. Instead, the AGRC concentrated its energies on "Search and Recovery"—the recovery and concentration of isolated and unrecorded burials and unburied remains.

Search and recovery efforts began as early as 1944 in some rearward areas and increased significantly in late 1945, when the AGRC was assigned primary responsibility for carrying out the postwar Casualty Clearance Plan.[3] The plan was designed to confirm or alter the casualty status (Presumed Dead, Missing in Action, Missing, Prisoner of War, or Captured) provisionally assigned during the war to thousands of American soldiers. Because the families of these men anxiously awaited word on the status of their military kin, casualty clearance was given high priority. To hasten the process, the AGRC undertook the responsibility of finding the recorded and reported burials of American military casualties, and also made searches for the locations of graves of all individuals believed to be deceased. Time was critical, since the shorter the time between death and burial in a registered grave, the likelier was the possibility of a positive identification.

The European search and recovery mission was accomplished by a series of area sweeps, each of which was carried out in three phases. In the first phase a three-man Propaganda Team systematically visited communities in a given area, distributing posters describing the search and recovery operation and urging local people to come forward with any information they might have regarding burial places of American dead. Appeals to local residents to contact the team were also publicized in radio broadcasts, posters displayed in public places, and newspaper announcements.

The early data-gathering phase was followed by the time-consuming investigative phase, when a special team followed every lead concerning the whereabouts of American grave sites. All investigations began with data contained in digests of documented cases compiled by Command Headquarters. The digests were prepared from such sources as Casualty Clearance Plan forms,

American Graves Registration Command: European Area. The Central
Identification Point (CIP) at Strasbourg and the route home of Lieutenant
Wood's remains has been added to the map (from Steere and Boardman
1957: 224)

Missing Air Crew Reports, and German Green Cards and Buff Cards. The latter two cards were prepared by the German government for enemy soldiers who died in German prison hospitals, and records of prisoners of war who were treated in German prison hospitals, and for those killed in crash landings behind German lines.

Arriving in a locality with these reports in hand, the Investigating Team contacted community leaders and other residents who were reported to have information on burial places of American soldiers. Further clues were gleaned from hospital and cemetery records and from the files in mayors' offices. All documented cases were researched until the graves in question were found, or it was shown that the sites could not be found. The team was obliged to continue its investigations until it had thoroughly inquired into every rumor and bit of gossip about the disposition of American remains for which no documentary evidence existed.

The final phase of search and recovery was accomplished by the Disinterring Team, consisting of an investigator, a driver-disinterment medic, and several local laborers. This team used the information gathered during the previous phase to go to the grave site and exhume the remains, which were then removed to mobile collecting points for transfer to cemeteries in the liberated countries: France, Belgium, The Netherlands, or Luxembourg. No American war dead were to be permanently buried in countries with which America had been at war, so all casualties were removed from German soil. In contrast, all British war dead traditionally remain in the country in which they died.

For nearly three and a half years, search and recovery units continued to make sweeps, and in some areas re-sweeps, of Europe in quest of isolated remains. That part of northern Europe where American troops had been in combat was divided into four zones for this purpose. Germany itself was a fifth zone, under the First Field Command, and Italy was in the Mediterranean Zone, a separate area command. When AGRC field activities ended in 1949, 16,584 isolated remains had been recovered throughout

Europe from the ephemeral Nazi empire. The British, French, and American zones in what was to become West Germany had been swept repeatedly.

Between November 1945 and June 1946, a winter operation conducted in 73,153 square miles from southern Germany to the North Sea and its offshore islands yielded 6,220 American casualties in isolated graves. AGRC Headquarters was not satisfied with the search, for its results had fallen short of expectations and another re-sweep of 93,000 square miles in western Germany was planned and carried out between July 1946 through 1947. Many cases investigated were those based on information obtained by repeated appeals to local citizens. The First Field Command in Germany had twenty-seven search teams and twelve recovery teams in the field.

Red Army regulations on searches for airmen in East Germany were consistently hampered by restrictions that had no overt purpose except to restrict access to the area. Only cases related to war crimes were at first permitted by the Soviets, although eventually 311 American casualties were recovered from behind what was to become the Iron Curtain.

At first, disinterment teams tried to identify the remains at the graveside, as they had done during the years of combat, but this left a great deal to be desired. The disinterring team usually stood idle while the leader conducted his investigation regarding the identity of the casualty. Then, too, these individuals were usually not competent to make the type of decisions their work called upon them to make. For these reasons, the decision was made to evacuate the remains to a central identification point where the work could be done by specialists.

*　　*　　*

The search and recovery efforts were highly successful, but the mission was never intended to be an end in itself. The success of the postwar graves registration program was measured by the rate

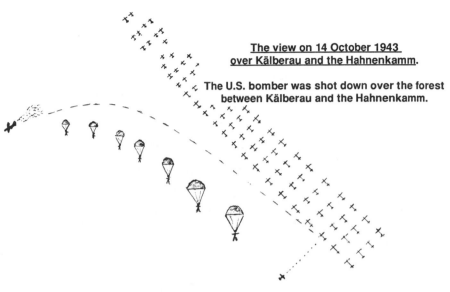

So sah es am 14. Oktober 1943
über Kälberau und dem Hahnenkamm aus.

Über dem Wald zwischen Kälberau und dem
Hahnenkamm wurde der US Bomber abgeschossen.

The view on 14 October 1943
over Kälberau and the Hahnenkamm.

**The U.S. bomber was shot down over the forest
between Kälberau and the Hahnenkamm.**

Observation tower on
the Hahnenkamm

Man who lost his foot

Dowden

Plane hit here

Eyewitnesses to the shooting down of the _Wicked WAAC_ over the town of
Kälberau provided this graphic version of the event, and the landing places
of two of its crew. The view is south. (Courtesy of Rudi Kress)

CONFIDENTIAL

SECRET
AUTH: CE :6RG
DATE
INITIALS:

Classification changed
to.....RESTRICTED......
by E. A. BRADUNAS, Lt. Col., AC
by F. M. MUENCH, Capt., AC
Date.... MAR 1 1946

WAR DEPARTMENT
HEADQUARTERS ARMY AIR FORCES
WASHINGTON

MISSING AIR CREW REPORT

Classification changed
to: CONFIDENTIAL
Auth:
Init:
Date: 21 Oct 43

o.K.
821

IMPORTANT: This report will be compiled in triplicate by each Army Air
Forces organization within 48 hours of the time an aircraft is
officially reported missing.

1. ORGANIZATION: Location **AAF Station 111** ; Command or Air Force **8th**
Group **306th Bomb Gp(H)** ; Squadron **369th Bomb Sq.** XXXXXXXX
2. SPECIFY: Point of Departure **Thurleigh, England** ; Course **as Prescribed**
Intended Destination **Schweinfurt, England** Type of Mission **H. Bomb**
3. WEATHER CONDITIONS AND VISIBILITY AT TIME OF CRASH OR WHEN LAST REPORTED:
oct Hazy
4. GIVE: (a)Date **14/10/43** ;Time **Unknown** , and Location **Unknown**
of last known whereabouts of missing aircraft.
(b) Specify whether ( ) Last Sighted; ( ) Last contacted by Radio;
( ) Forced Down; ( ) Seen to Crash; or (x) Information not Available.
5. AIRCRAFT WAS LOST, OR IS BELIEVED TO HAVE BEEN LOST, AS A RESULT OF: (Check only
one (x)Enemy Aircraft; ( ) Enemy Anti-Aircraft; ( ) Other Circumstances as
follows _____
6. AIRCRAFT: Type, Model and Series **B-17F** ; A.A.F. Serial Number **42-30199**
7. ENGINES: Type, Model and Series **R 1820-97** A.A.F. Serial Number(a) **43-57662**
(b) **43-58007** ;(c) **43-58110** ;(d) **43-57743**
8. INSTALLED WEAPONS (Furnish below Make, Type and Serial Number)
(a) **F-383036** ; (b) **F-383250** ; (c) **F-382985** ; (d) **KH-145622**
(e) **F-383450** ; (f) **F-383395** ; (g) **F-383228** ; (h) **S-119917**
9. THE PERSONS LISTED BELOW WERE REPORTED AS: (a) Battle Casualty **x**
XXXXXXXXXXXXXXXXXXXX
10. NUMBER OF PERSONS ABOARD AIRCRAFT: Crew **10** ;Passengers **0** ;Total **10**
(Starting with pilot, furnish the following particulars; If more than 10
persons were aboard aircraft, list similar particulars on separate sheet
and attach original to this form).

	Crew Position	Name in Full (Last Name First)	Rank	Serial Number
EUS 1.	Pilot	Bettinger, George C.	1st Lt.	O-733592
EUS 2.	Co-Pilot	Block, Abraham	2nd Lt.	O-736085
KIA 3.	Navigator	Wood, Elbert S. Jr.	2nd Lt.	O-683365
RTD 4.	Bombardier	Dowden, Leland A.	2nd Lt.	O-676577
EUS 5.	Top Turret Gunner	Gerking, Samuel F.	S/Sgt.	39303948
EUS 6.	Radio Operator	Lewis, Gordon F.	S/Sgt.	39828747
EUS 7.	Ball Turret Gunner	Mills, Elmer W.	T/Sgt.	32399676
EUS 8.	Right Waist Gunner	Montana, James F.	S/Sgt.	36349974
EUS 9.	Left Waist Gunner	Williams, Donald R.	S/Sgt.	17034562
EUS 10.	Tail Gunner	Voight, Linden K.	S/Sgt.	37372321

11. IDENTIFY BELOW THOSE PERSONS WHO ARE BELIEVED TO HAVE LAST KNOWLEDGE OF AIR-
CRAFT, AND CHECK APPROPRIATE COLUMN TO INDICATE BASIS FOR SAME.

			Contacted			Saw
Name in Full (Last Name First)	Rank	Serial Number	By Radio	Last Sighted	Saw Crash	Forced Landing
1. None						
2.						
3.						

12. IF PERSONNEL ARE BELIEVED TO HAVE SURVIVED, ANSWER YES TO ONE OF THE FOLLOWING
STATEMENTS: (a) Parachutes were used ; (b)Persons were seen walking away from scene of crash ;or(c) Any other reason(Specify) **Unknown**
13. ATTACH AERIAL PHOTOGRAPH,MAP,CHART,OR SKETCH,SHOWING APPROXIMATE LOCATION WHERE
AIRCRAFT WAS LAST SEEN.
14. ATTACH EYEWITNESS DESCRIPTION OF CRASH,FORCED LANDING,OR OTHER CIRCUMSTANCES
PERTAINING TO MISSING AIRCRAFT.
15. ATTACH A DESCRIPTION OF THE EXTENT OF SEARCH, IF ANY, AND GIVE NAME, RANK AND
SERIAL NUMBER OF OFFICER IN CHARGE HERE **None**

Reverse Side.
SECRET
Reproduced by
Hq. 306th Bomb Gp(H); 14 July/43.

Date of Report **15 October 1943.**

(Signature of Preparing Officer)
(PAUL J. BAILLIE, 1st Lt., Air Corps,
Asst. Adjutant, 306th Bomb Gp(H).

Missing Air Crew Report No. 821, reporting the loss of the *Wicked WAAC*
during the Second Schweinfurt raid. (National Archives: Suitland)

Above: A pre-war view of Michelbach from the north slope of the Hahnenkamm. (Photograph by Christian Hübner)

Below: The track of the *Wicked WAAC* after being struck over the town of Kälberau. The view is to the southwest. (Courtesy of Rudi Kress)

Germans inspect a downed Flying Fortress. (Courtesy of Squadron/Signal
Publications)

Above: Air view of the landing site of Lieutenant Wood on the bank of the Kahl River between Kälberau and Michelbach; the view is to the northeast.

Right: Andreas Noll, 1876–1970, Bürgermeister of Michelbach, 1912–1945. (Photograph courtesy of Rudi Kress)

Nr. 10

C

Geiselbach , den 15.Oktober 1943

Der Wagner Heinrich R i e n e c k e r
, katholisch

wohnhaft in Geiselbach Hausnummer 76

ist am 14.Oktober 1943 um 14 Uhr 30 Minuten

in Geiselbach , Flurgemarkung Omersbacherweg verstorben.

Der Verstorbene war geboren am 23.Oktober 1899

in Geiselbach

(Standesamt Geiselbach Nr. 23)

Vater: Peter Rienecker
Wagner

Mutter: Maria Magdalena Rienecker
geborene Thoma

Der Verstorbene war ledig verheiratet mit der noch lebenden
Rosa Rienecker geborene Weber

Eingetragen auf mündliche schriftliche Anzeige des Vaters des Verstorbenen

Der Anzeigende ist bekannt

Vorstehend zwei Druckworte gestrichen

Vorgelesen, genehmigt und unterschrieben

Der Standesbeamte

Todesursache: Plötzlicher Tod, schwere Gehirnerschütterung, mit
schweren Verbrennungen am Kopf u.Rücken durch Flugzeugex-
plosion, komplizierter Beinbruch u.mehere Wunden an den Bei

Beglaubigung des Verstorbenen am 25.10.1928 in Geiselbach

(Standesamt Geiselbach Nr. 13).

Above: The old fire station at Michelbach. Since there was no morgue in Michelbach in 1943, Lieutenant Wood's body was kept here until his funeral.

Left: The death certificate of Wagner Peter Rienecker, who was killed by the crash of the *Wicked WAAC*. He died instantly of a brain concussion and other injuries. (Courtesy of Erich Henkel)

Newspaper headlines from the *Aschaffenburger Zeitung* in the days following Second Schweinfurt. Top to bottom: "Blackest Day for the USA Bombers"; "Parachutes Hanging in Clusters in the Air"; "The Flying Coffins of the Americans"; "The German Air Defense 'Too Well Organized'"; and "Five Heavy Bombers in 45 Minutes." This aerial victory of the Luftwaffe provided a needed, if temporary, boost to German morale after the carnage the Wehrmacht had suffered in Russia, and the collapse of Italy following the loss of North Africa and Sicily.

Luftwaffe flight log of Herbert Schob from August 16 to November 5, 1943. The entry for flight 2,234 claims "1 Boeing 17 Fortress shot down in flames E. Frankfurt 2:10 pm." Was this the *Wicked WAAC?* (Courtesy of Werner Girbig)

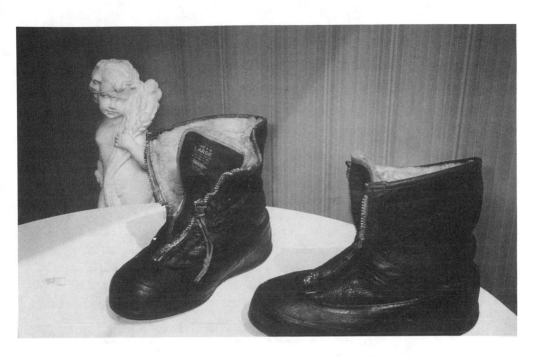

Above: Lieutenant Wood's A-6 fleece-lined flight boots. They were given to the author in 1991. The name "Wood" had been worn off the toe of the right boot by years of post-war use. The zippers are broken and the fleece is worn but they are otherwise in excellent condition. (Courtesy of Rudi Kress)

Below: Luftgaukommando "Buff Card" for Lieutenant Wood. (United States Army)

Gefangenenlager: *KN 323*	Staatsangehörigkeit: *U.S.A.*	Nr. der Liste: *0-683,363*
Gefangenen-Nr.: *1/2 Wood Elbert S. Jr.*		Seite der Liste: *agne*
Name: *Wood (0-683,365)*		Beruf:
		Religion:
Vornamen: *Elbert S. jr.*		Dienstgrad: *2 Ltn 2nd*

Geburtstag u. Geburtsort:	Truppenteil: *Masch. Fortress*
Vorname des Vaters:	Komp. usw. Matr. Nr. *0-683 363*
Familienname der Mutter:	Ort und Tag der Gefangennahme oder Internierung: *K.I.A.*
Name u. Anschrift der zu benachrichtigenden Person:	Verwundungen, Verletzungen oder Tod: *14 Okt. 43*
	wann und von wo zugegangen: *owria ?*

Aufenthalt u. Veränderungen: *Fl 14. 10. 43*

Grablage:
K - 14 okt. 43 E 70

W.D., A.G.O. FORM . 54.

WOOD,   ELBERT S. JR.,   0-683365   Missing   a 2nd t.,
(Last name) (First name) (Initial) (A.S.N.)   (Grade)

369th Bombardment Squadron (H) : 306th Bombardment Group (H)
(Organization or Arm or Service)

Missing in Action

who ~~died~~ on the 14 day of October , 19 43 .

CLASS I—Saber, insignia, decorations, medals, campaign badges, watches, manuscripts, and other articles valuable chiefly as keepsakes.	CLASS II—Other effects., (cont.)
NO. ARTICLES	NO. ARTICLES
1 Stamp Collection	2 Article Kits
1 Writing Portfolio	12 pr Socks
3 Pipes	1 Polo Shirts
1 201 File	1 Gym Pants
1 Photograph	1 Brush
3 Insignia U.S.	1 Bag of Laundry
2 Insignia A.C.	1 Battle Jacket.
1 Service Ribbon	
1 Coin Collection	A. BENEFICIARY:
	MR. E. S. WOOD. (FATHER)
	CODY, NEBRASKA.
	B. NO CREDITORS
	C. NO DEBTORS
	D. NO BANKING ACCOUNT IN THE UK.
CLASS II— Other effects.	
NO. ARTICLES	
5 Shirts	
6 Trousers	
2 Blouses	
3 pr Shoes	
1 Gym Suit	
3 Towels	
5 Ties	
3 Flight Cap	

Money   (Specie $ None
          (Notes ¢ None

I CERTIFY that the foregoing inventory comprises all the effects of the
~~deceased~~ Missing whose name appears on the first page hereof, and that the effects were
delivered to _Q.M.S.O. ADVANCED AIR DEPOT NO. 2., APO 635._

(Give name and degree of relationship; if legal representative or
beneficiary named by the deceased, so state.)

AAF STATION # 111   DUDLEY D. ALLEN,
(Station)   1st Lt.,   AC,
                         Investigating Officer.

22 November , 1943
(Date)

* Strike out words not applicable.   Repd.Hq, 306th Bomb.Gp., 10 Aug. 1943

Inventory of Lieutenant Wood's personal effects, as recorded at AAF Station
111, Thurleigh, England. Filed on November 22, 1943—five and a half weeks
after Black Thursday. They did not reach his parents in Nebraska until
mid-October 1944. (United States Army)

A 423rd Bomb Squadron personnel hut at Thurleigh, abandoned for nearly half a century.

Above: Death certificate of Elbert S. Wood, filed in Michelbach on July 14, 1949, by Andreas Noll. (Archives of Stadt Alzenau in Unterfranken, Bavaria, Germany)

Below: The *Wicked WAAC* seconds before its destruction on the Omersbach-Geiselbach road. (Watercolor painting by James C. Fisher)

Above: The Catholic cemetery in Michelbach. Lieutenant Wood was buried to the right of the white stone cross in the far right background.

Right: Sketch of the Catholic cemetery at Michelbach, made by the War Graves Registration Command disinterring team on March 13, 1947. (United States Army)

CEMETERY of MICHELBACH
(L-51/M-96)

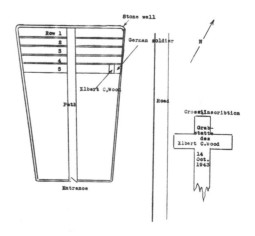

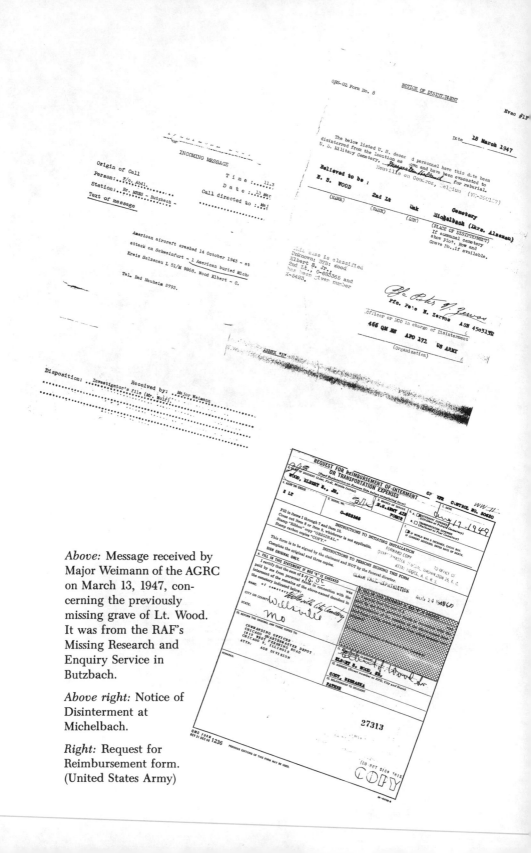

Above: Message received by Major Weimann of the AGRC on March 13, 1947, concerning the previously missing grave of Lt. Wood. It was from the RAF's Missing Research and Enquiry Service in Butzbach.

Above right: Notice of Disinterment at Michelbach.

Right: Request for Reimbursement form. (United States Army)

CLASS OF SERVICE		SYMBOLS
This is a full-rate Telegram or Cablegram unless its deferred character is indicated by a suitable symbol above or preceding the address.		DL=Day Letter
		NL=Night Letter
		LC=Deferred Cable
		NLT=Cable Night Letter
		Ship Radiogram

WESTERN UNION

1201

A. N. WILLIAMS
PRESIDENT

The filing time shown in the date line on telegrams and day letters is STANDARD TIME at point of origin. Time of receipt is STANDARD TIME at point of destination

WM W 44 govt WUX Washington D C 1133 am Oct 26 1943

Elbert S Wood Sr

Cody Nebr.

The secretary of war desires me to express his regret that your son second Lieut Elbert S Wood Jr has been reported missing in action since fourteen October over Schwienfurt Germany if further details or other information are recieved you will be promptl y notified.

Ulio The Adt General
1146 am

THE COMPANY WILL APPRECIATE SUGGESTIONS FROM ITS PATRONS CONCERNING ITS SERVICE

CLASS OF SERVICE		SYMBOLS
This is a full-rate Telegram or Cablegram unless its deferred character is indicated by a suitable symbol above or preceding the address.		DL=Day Letter
		NL=Night Letter
		LC=Deferred Cable
		NLT=Cable Night Letter
		Ship Radiogram

WESTERN UNION

1204

A. N. WILLIAMS
PRESIDENT

The filing time shown in the date line on telegrams and day letters is STANDARD TIME at point of origin. Time of receipt is STANDARD TIME at point of destination

WM W 48 Govt Washington D C D 740p m Jan 1 1943

Elbbert S Wood Sr,

Cody Nebr.

Report received from the German Government through the International Red Cross states your son second Lieut Elbert S Wood Jr who was previously reported missing in action was killed in action on fourteenth Octobert in the European area the secretary of war extends his deepest sympathy letter follows .

Ulio The adj General .
828 pm

THE COMPANY WILL APPRECIATE SUGGESTIONS FROM ITS PATRONS CONCERNING ITS SERVICE

Telegrams from Major General J. A. Ulio, the Adjutant General of the United States, announcing that Lieutenant Wood was Missing in Action, and Killed in Action.

The American cemetery at Neuville-en-Condroz, Belgium, June 27, 1946, as the first graves are being dug and filled. (Courtesy of the Smithsonian Institution)

of identification of American war dead. Under the "Return of the Dead Program," more commonly known as "repatriation," next of kin were given the option of having the remains interred in a permanent United States military cemetery overseas or having them returned to the United States for burial in a national or private cemetery. Clearly, the goals of the repatriation program could be achieved only if bodies were positively identified, in which cases families could be contacted for their decision on final disposition of the remains.

In the early months of search and recovery, AGRC field units made every effort to identify isolated burials and unburied remains as they were recovered. The disinterring teams tried to establish the identity of exhumed remains at the grave site, usually based on one or more of the following: (1) an identification tag worn around the neck, (2) an identification tag found elsewhere on or near the person, (3) a paybook found in the clothing, (4) an Emergency Medical Tag signed by a medical officer and fastened to the body, or (5) an identification bracelet worn around the wrist.

Exhumed bodies were removed to mobile collecting points that had personnel and facilities for attempting even the most difficult identification problems. There, field identifications were confirmed and unidentified remains underwent a thorough examination for more clues that might reveal the identity of the individual.[4] Initially, this procedure was reasonably effective. But, as the months wore on, the increasing time lag between death and recovery of the body made the task of identifying unknown remains more and more difficult.

The AGRC sought out expert advice in several areas to help them identify unknown remains, including that from detectives and from specialists in physical anthropology. Early in 1946, Dr. Harry L. Shapiro, Curator of Physical Anthropology at the American Museum of Natural History in New York, received a telephone call from the Quartermaster General in Washington, DC, and was asked if he could be of help in the identification of the war dead. Assuring the Quartermaster General that "current knowledge of skeletal variation and its correlations with age, sex and race would be helpful," Shapiro was asked to visit sites in Europe where American casualties were being exhumed and to study the identification problems faced by the AGRC. Shapiro went to France in May of 1946 and began a three- to four-month tour of Western Europe, ending his visit in Austria. He then offered a set of recommendations for means of identifying the war dead based on techniques of physical anthropology.[5]

The techniques recommended by Shapiro were quickly put into practice at the newly created Central Identification Point (CIP), established in a military barracks in Strasbourg, France. The personnel at the CIP responsible for the identification in Europe were European forensic scientists under the technical direction of C. Simonin. No American scientists were employed there. Beginning on August 7, 1946, and until the late spring of 1947, all recovered remains, both known and unknown, plus personal effects and other identifying media, were first sent directly to the CIP, 349 Quartermaster Battalion, APO 154, for a complete examination. A second CIP was later established at Neuville-en-Condroz, Belgium, where the activities, under the direction of F. Vandervael of the University of Liège, paralleled those at Strasbourg. The Belgian CIP handled all the remains found in isolated locations, and in addition it reprocessed all unknowns who had been buried up to that time in cemeteries throughout The Netherlands and Belgium.

Other avenues for identification were also exploited. John Aievoli, a detective in the New York Police Department, was one of the outstanding civilian contributors to early identification efforts in the European Theater. His recommendations for techniques and procedures, drawn from years of homicide investigations in New York, greatly expedited the identification of the dead. He served in the European Theater until mid-October 1946. Officials in the OQMG who praised his contributions to the program "considered his efforts among the most helpful of any individual in the entire European GRS organization."

Processing of remains was a complex task done by a team of technicians using a variety of analytical techniques, including skeletal reconstruction, determination of race, age and stature, dental charting, and fingerprinting. It began with the arrival of the remains at the CIP, when workers delivered the mortuary box to the processing laboratory. The accompanying paperwork was carefully reviewed by technicians before the remains were taken to a processing table covered by a clean mattress cover. A team consisting of a table supervisor and three assistants, one of them a recorder, began their examination. These men possessed a variety of skills: they knew enough about the human body to reconstruct the skeleton, to make an accurate tooth chart, and to take fingerprints under difficult conditions.

The initial search generally revealed the identification tags were missing, especially for those casualties who had been in German hands. The size, serial number, and the trademark on undergarments were examined, as were all personal objects, which were forwarded to the personal effects section. Objects carrying clues that were effaced or unreadable were sent to the chemistry laboratory for further analysis. The Chemical Laboratory in Strasbourg continued its activities until late spring 1947, when it was moved to the Fontainebleau Depot near Paris. A Photographic Laboratory also was established to photograph clues found by the investigating team, and used an infrared lamp to photograph faded writing and laundry marks.[6]

Following a thorough physical examination of the remains, the body was fluoroscoped, a process that often revealed identification tags, bracelets, rings, and other metallic objects that otherwise might not have been found. Fluoroscopic or chemical analysis of clothing also sometimes yielded clues to the identify of the individual. Mass burials and extremely fragmentary remains proved challenging, but even so, positive identifications could sometimes be made.

After compiling their files, the CIP sent the body to one of the American cemeteries in Europe. The information was then forwarded to Headquarters, AGRC, for assessment and, where possible, identification. The principal role of the CIP was not to identify the remains, but to collect the data necessary to help in identification.

After his return to the United States, Harry Shapiro was periodically notified that problematic cases that could not be resolved at the CIP had arrived at the Brooklyn Navy Yard for him to inspect. He was able to provide identities for some of these cases.

The skill and persistence of the CIP technicians is shown by the fact that of over 148,000 remains recovered in the European Theater, only slightly more than 1,700—just over one percent—remained unidentified at the close of the graves registration program at the end of 1951. On a worldwide basis, 281,000 bodies had been recovered and only 10,000, slightly over 3.5 percent, were unidentified. Identification efforts continued even after the program ended, however, and by 1954 this figure had fallen to 3.1 percent.

On October 10, 1947, the bodies of 3,012 war dead were returned to the United States from the Pacific Theater aboard the United States Army Transport *Honda Knot*. This event marked the beginning of the Return of the Dead program. Later that month the first war dead repatriated from the European zones—6,248 men—arrived aboard the Army Transport *Joseph V. Connolly*. In time, the remains of more than 171,000 of those who died overseas during World War II were returned to American soil. Although there was debate in the popular press about the pros and cons of the Return of the Dead program, next of kin of more than half the recovered dead preferred they be returned to the United States for burial. The total cost of the program was about $157,986,000, an average cost of $564.50 for each casualty.

Each casualty processed by the GRS and AGRC generated a dossier known as a "293 file"—the individual deceased personnel file. These files are now held by the Mortuary Affairs and Casualty Division, United States Army Military Personnel Center, Alexandria, Virginia.

Recent efforts to identify the remains of Vietnam War casualties are today the responsibility of the United States Army Central Identification Laboratory (CIL), at Fort Shafter, Hawaii. CIL personnel continue to identify World War II casualties that come to their attention, as well as those from Korea and Southeast Asia. Modern methods of forensic anthropology in use today are capable of identifying anyone—through a combination of skeletal analysis, blood type, and DNA. Given the proper documentation, there will be no "Unknown Soldier" in some future conflict.

CHAPTER ELEVEN
A MELANCHOLY HOMECOMING

The 466th Quartermaster Battalion had begun service on the Continent at Carentan, Normandy, on the boundary between Omaha and Utah beaches, and had followed the trail of casualties across France and into Germany until, in the spring of 1947, it was based in Kassel. The pace of its recovery activity was beginning to wind down by that time and things were slack. On the afternoon of the same day the message was received from the Missing Research and Enquiry Service, Major Gustave Weimann of the AGRC sent Gaston Wolf to investigate the case of the American flier buried in the cemetery at Michelbach, ninety miles southwest of Kassel.[1]

Wolf's first visit was to the Bürgermeister of Michelbach, Oskar Grünzfelder, who had assumed office after Andreas Noll's dismissal. Grünzfelder told Wolf that on the day of the Schweinfurt mission he'd seen a burning plane in the direction of Geiselbach, northeast of town, and that he had seen fliers descending in parachutes. They landed, he said, between Michelbach and Kälberau. Grünzfelder gave Wolf a certified copy of a statement made on Sunday, January 6, 1946, by Noll, and took Wolf for the short walk from the city hall to Lieutenant Wood's grave.

They walked into the cemetery and down a central path toward a life-sized statue of Christ on the cross and turned right. The grave lay in the shade of one of the trees that line the cemetery

wall that, on the north, shields the visitor's view of the famous
Weingut Höfler winery in the adjoining lots. The disinterring team,
under the direction of Wolf's assistant, Pfc. Peter N. Zervos, with
the help of four German laborers, immediately began opening the
grave. As part of the documentation of the event, Pfc. Zervos also
made a sketch of the location of the grave in the cemetery.

That evening Wolf interviewed Andreas Noll. The former
Bürgermeister had written the 1946 statement, Wolf said, "for his
own protection" about the burial of the flier Noll called "C. W.
Wood." Dr. Ludwig Reichert also prepared a statement eleven days
later, on January 17. Noll told Wolf that "C. W. Wood" was the
name given him by the German medical officer (*Stabsarzt*). When
he was asked why there was no entry in the cemetery register on
the burial, Noll explained that the *Stabsarzt* had told him no entry
was to be made, and he obeyed the order. In fact, it was not until
July 14, 1949—more than two years after his disinterment—that
Noll, as the Registrar, entered a note, registered as Death No. 21
for 1943, in the Bureau of Vital Statistics in the Registry Office,
or Standesamt, at Michelbach that passes for a death certificate for
Lieutenant Wood.

Noll's 1946 statement says that several fliers from a burning
plane came down near Michelbach by parachute. Among these
men, as his identification tag showed, was a "C. W. Wood," whom
witnesses said was already dead when he landed. There was a
rumor in the village that the airman was a Canadian, a rumor that
had reached the British MRES unit in Butzbach. When their
investigation of the incident found that the airman was not an RAF
casualty, they notified the AGRC of their discovery. Noll told Wolf
how later he saw the flier lying in Michelbach beside the road to
Kälberau, having been brought there by Luftwaffe personnel and
by local French prisoners.

Wolf also went to Alzenau, two miles southwest of Michelbach,
to obtain a statement from Dr. Reichert. Reichert's statement of
January 17 had been forwarded to the Office of Military Government at Alzenau. In it he detailed the examination he had made

of Lieutenant Wood's body in the Michelbach firehouse.

The disinterring team reached the coffin the next morning at a depth of six feet. No dog tags were found, nor was anything discovered in the navigator's pockets, since it was customary for the Germans to remove all such personal effects: they sent one identification tag to the Central Tracing Agency of the International Red Cross; the other, to Berlin. The body was fully clothed save for footwear. Lieutenant Wood's A-6 fleece-lined flight boots had been removed and, until they were given to this author in 1991, remained in the possession of the man who dug his grave in 1943.

The remains were placed in a metallic liner and mattress cover in a new burial box together with the wood cross. Before leaving, Pfc. Zervos left a "Notice of Disinterment" with the Bürgermeister. The remains were assigned "Evacuation No. 1F 3157" for removal to the United States Military Cemetery at the Subordinate Identification Point at Margraten, in The Netherlands. From that point they were transferred to Neuville-en-Condroz, the military cemetery and Central Identification Point in the Ardennes region near Liège in Belgium.

The only German records available about Lieutenant Wood are "D/L 16/66" and "RUS 3040-3059," both of which incorrectly list the final digit of his service number as 3 instead of 5.

D/L 16/66: *"Elbert S. Wood Jr.; 2. Leutn.; 0-683363; 14.10.43; Grablage: noch nicht gemeldet"* [Grave site: not yet reported].

RUS 3040-3059: *"KU 323; 14.10.1943; 2. Nachmeldung zu L.P. Nr. 104 966/43 vom 8.11.1943; Wood, Elbert S. Jr.; 2. Lt.; Erk. Marke [Erkennungsmarke]: 0-683363; tot."* [KU 323; October 14, 1943; Confirmation of L.P. No. 104 966/43 of November 8, 1943; Wood, Elbert S., Jr.; 2nd Lt.; Army Serial Number 0-683-363; dead.]

*   *   *

There were two discrepancies in the identification that called for investigation at Neuville-en-Condroz. Not only were there inconsistencies in the name (C. W. Wood and Elbert C. Wood versus Elbert S. Wood), but the number "7934" that was marked on some of the clothing did not agree with Wood's army serial number. For this reason the remains were classified as Unknown X-5423: "Unknown, BTB [believed to be]: Wood, Elbert S. Jr., 2nd Lt., 0-683365," as listed in the American Graves Registration Command Casualties Book.

An "Identification Check List" was processed at the CIP by Ernest C. Gaddy, Chief Warrant Officer, on April 24, 1947. This form noted the remains were clothed in an officer's pink shirt and green trousers, tie, yellow web belt, cotton socks, jockey shorts, and size 40 one-piece gabardine A4 flying coveralls. Leather bars denoting the rank of second lieutenant were on the coverall shoulders and the name "E. S. Wood" was printed on the left chest. There were no shoes. The fluoroscopic examination was negative, that is, no foreign matter was detected. A careful comparison also was made by Harold D. Wheeler, A.D., of the tooth charts prepared for X-5423 and the dental records made for Wood in June of 1943. The two records corresponded in all essential particulars, and the few minor discrepancies were easily reconciled. For example, one of Lieutenant Wood's teeth recorded in June 1943 as "missing" was found to be "not fully erupted" in X-5423.

Laboratory examination began at Neuville to help resolve the identification. The results of "Chemical Laboratory Case No. 1366" were reported on Friday, May 9, 1947. Roland A. Korba, Identification Technician, recorded that the laboratory found the numeral "7934" stenciled eight times on the waist band of the pair of jockey-type cotton shorts worn by X-5423 (Hanes Sports, size 28). This number, found on two other items of clothing, corresponded to the last four digits of Wood's enlisted serial number (ASN 170 3 7934).

The remains were then temporarily reinterred at Neuville-en-Condroz pending the result of the identification processes begun there. The Report of Interment filed on May 20, 1947, states the remains were buried in a casket at Neuville at 3:00 p.m. on that date in Plot V, Row 11, Grave No. 267, and marked by a temporary wood cross. A joint Protestant, Catholic, and Hebrew religious ceremony was conducted by Chaplains Rusher, Saatman, and Lepchivcher, respectively. Such ceremonies were customary when the identification of the deceased was in doubt. Military honors, however, were not conducted, since this was not customary when temporary interments were made in military cemeteries overseas.

*   *   *

Wood's family was growing impatient at having heard nothing about Elbert's whereabouts. On October 10, Lieutenant Wood's mother wrote a letter to the Quartermaster General, asking for information on her son's grave, since she believed "ample time has passed" for it to have been found. The delay, of course, lay in the volume of paperwork that was demanded by the identification process for him and for thousands of other casualties.

Only a month before, on September 12, 1947, the Memorial Division of the Quartermaster Corps in Washington had asked the Records Administration Center in St. Louis, Missouri, to provide them with forms for Lieutenant Wood. The St. Louis office complied with the request on October 16. On October 31 they also complied with a second request from the Memorial Division and forwarded a copy of the report of Lieutenant Wood's physical examination, including dental records made on June 24, 1943, two days before his graduation from navigation school at San Marcos.

The Memorial Division replied to the letter of Wood's mother on December 2, 1947, in a communication that said "although no conclusive information is available as to the recovery and the identification of the remains of your son, remains have been recovered and interred in the U.S. Military Cemetery Neuville-en-Condroz, Belgium, and which may be those of your loved one. An investigation is now being conducted in order to determine beyond a shadow of a doubt, the identify of those remains. Upon conclusion of this investigation you will be informed of the results."

On November 16, 1948, a three-member board of review met

at the Headquarters, AGRC, European Theater, to evaluate the records accumulated on X-5423. It consisted of Major Robert E. Deppe and Captains Jack C. Hayes and Burge A. Wiemeyer. This board accepted the accumulated evidence that the remains of X-5423 were those of 2nd Lieutenant Elbert S. Wood.

"Unknown X-5423" was identified through (1) the excellent agreement between his tooth chart and that recorded in the Office of the Quartermaster General; (2) the laundry mark "7934," found three times on the clothing of X-5423 and eight times on his briefs, was consistent with the last four digits of the enlisted serial number of Lieutenant Wood when he was an aviation cadet; (3) the name "E. S. Wood" was found on the flying coveralls of X-5423; (4) the two leather 2nd lieutenant's bars found on his coveralls were in agreement with Wood's rank; (5) the estimated date and place of death of X-5423 was consistent with the Missing Air Crew Report for B-17 Serial No. 42-30199, of which Wood was a crew member; (6) the inscription on the cross on the grave in Michelbach read *"Grabstätte des Elbert C. Wood, 14 Oktober 1943"*; and (7) the records at Michelbach listed one American as being interred in that cemetery. In addition, the officer's shirt and trousers of X-5423 substantiated his rank as an officer.

On January 24, the Office of the Quartermaster General accepted the identification of the board of review and asked that "all records be amended accordingly."

*   *   *

On December 14, 1948, Headquarters, American Graves Registration Command, European Area, forwarded a corrected copy of the "Report of Burial" to the Quartermaster General in Washington, DC. The information in that document was then summarized in a letter by Major James F. Smith of the Quartermaster Corps Memorial Division to Wood's parents, dated February 8, 1949. The letter went on to say that "these remains have now been casketed and are being held" at Neuville-en-Condroz "pending disposition instructions from the next of kin, either for return to the United States or for permanent burial in an overseas cemetery," and that "There are inclosed informational pamphlets regarding the Return of World War II Dead Program, including a Disposition Form on which the father may indicate his desires in this matter. Upon receipt of the properly completed form, you may be assured that the Department of the Army will attempt to comply with your instructions as indicated thereon."

The choice to be reinterred in the United States instead of in foreign soil was one of more than 171,000 postwar decisions made by families of deceased servicemen. The "Request for Disposition of Remains," completed by Wood's father on February 17, directed that the remains be returned to Wellsville, Missouri, for burial. Although the family lived in Nebraska, several generations of Woods are buried there.

It was not inefficiency that led to the delays families found so frustrating as they awaited the return of their kin. A blizzard of paperwork was necessary to inventory the cemeteries so the War Department could successfully conduct a poll of the next of kin regarding their wishes. Storage facilities for the thousands of remains had to be created, not to mention the records necessary to process the receipt, inspection, repair, and transportation of caskets and shipping boxes.

Disinterring thousands of remains, checking their identifications, and transporting them to designated ports for shipment back to the United States also took time, particularly with the limited personnel available in Europe after the sudden, massive, and disorganized postwar demobilization of troops. All remains buried in temporary cemeteries had to be disinterred pending their return either to the United States or to a permanent cemetery overseas. The transfer and reinterment in permanent cemeteries in Europe of remains that were not repatriated also cut deeply into the time of the hard-pressed AGRC personnel.

Families were not aware, nor were they told, of these bureaucratic and logistic problems.[2] They simply awaited, with lessening

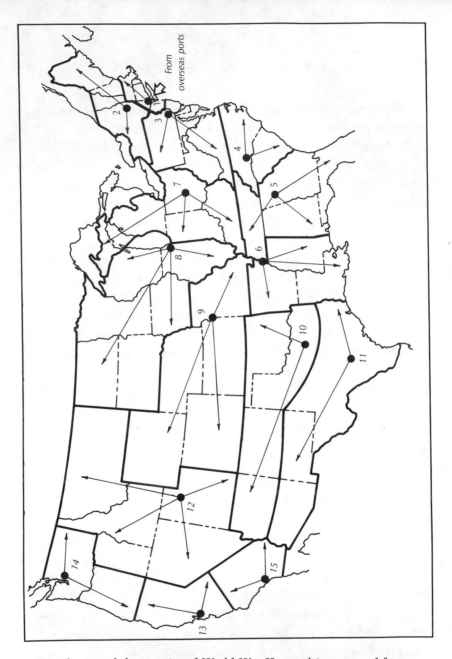

Distribution of the remains of World War II casualties returned from
overseas through the New York Port of Entry (Steere and Boardman).
There were fifteen distribution centers:

1. Brooklyn Army Base, New York
2. Schenectady General Depot
3. Philadelphia Quartermaster Depot
4. Charlotte Quartermaster Depot
5. Atlanta General Depot
6. Memphis General Depot
7. Columbus General Depot
8. Chicago Quartermaster Depot
9. Kansas City Quartermaster Depot
10. Fort Worth Quartermaster Depot
11. San Antonio General Depot
12. Utah General Depot
13. San Francisco Port
14. Auburn Sub-Depot (Seattle)
15. Mira Loma Quartermaster Depot
    (California)

patience, the return of their loved ones home. The first reparation ship did not leave Antwerp until the autumn of 1947.

One of nine copies prepared of the "Disinterment Directive," which was an order to disinter Elbert's remains, dated March 15, 1949, duly records that the remains of Lieutenant Wood earlier had been placed in a casket by Calvin Watson, Embalmer, on December 21, 1948, and that the casket was boxed and marked on December 28. The exterior finish on the first casket delivered was found to have a defective finish (it was blistered) and so was unsatisfactory for delivery of the remains to the United States. Another casket was used, and the defective one was taken to be repaired.

The "Record of Custodial Transfer" form records that on Saturday, May 28, 1949, Lieutenant Wood's casket was transported by truck by Corporal James H. Anderson from Neuville-en-Condroz to Pier 140 at the Belgian port of Antwerp. Three weeks later, on June 18, R. A. Salvador of the AGRC in Antwerp recorded that the casket was transferred into the hold of the United States Army Transport *Carroll Victory*. This "Victory" ship, built in 1944 in Los Angeles, was scheduled to carry thousands of repatriated war dead to the United States in 1948 and 1949. On June 28 the USAT *Carroll Victory* left Antwerp for the New York Port of Entry, flying the United States flag at half-mast during daylight hours.

The OQMG had chosen two cities—New York and San Francisco—to receive the repatriated remains from the European and Pacific theaters. Remains were then shipped from these ports to other distribution centers in trainload lots. Lieutenant Wood's flag-draped casket was shipped by rail, on July 19, to Distribution Center No. 8 at the Chicago Quartermaster Depot, Illinois. Elmond J. Miller was the train guard. From Chicago, the casket was shipped via the Wabash Railroad to Wellsville, a small town in east central Missouri. The train arrived at the Wellsville station on Wednesday, August 17, and the remains were taken to the Wells Funeral Home.

The casket of each repatriated casualty was accompanied from the distribution center to the man's hometown by a uniformed escort of the same branch of service, equal to or greater in rank than the deceased. Captain James F. McGraw was the military escort provided by the Quartermaster Corps for this occasion.

A funeral service was held by the Rev. J. C. McDaniel at the Wellsville Methodist Church the next day, followed by interment in the city cemetery. The day was typical of a Missouri summer—clear, hot, and humid, adding sweat and discomfort to the unhappy occasion. Full military honors were provided by Commander Paul Angel and members of the local Hayes-Hickerson Post No. 116 of the American Legion. The firing squad presented arms as the flag-draped casket was carried to the graveside.

At the conclusion of the minister's service, the pallbearers removed the flag from the casket and folded it. Captain McGraw presented the family with the flag, saying, "The Government of the United States presents to you, through the American Legion, the flag under which our comrade served." With the order "Ready, Load, Aim, Squad," and "Fire," three volleys by the firing squad echoed in the summer afternoon. Their echoes were followed by the melancholy notes of the bugler as "Taps" sounded across the cemetery. With "Order Arms," "Left Face," "At Trail," "Forward," and "March" the military escort disbanded and the funeral ended.

OQMG Form 1236, "Request for Reimbursement of Interment or Transportation Expenses," was filed by Elbert Wood, Sr., on August 17, 1949, in which he certified that "the sum of $75.00 was paid by me from personal funds in connection with the interment of the remains of the . . . decedent" in the Wellsville City Cemetery. An allowance not to exceed that amount was paid by the government toward the interment expenses of all repatriated World War II dead.

With the reimbursement of these funds the official file closes on the brief Army Air Force career of 2nd Lieutenant Elbert S. Wood. His only monument is a modest gray tombstone bearing his engraved name and rank, his bomb group and squadron designation, and a navigator's wings. Physically, it is a mirror image of the adjoining one of Elbert S. Wood, Sr., who died twenty-seven years after his son.

CHAPTER TWELVE
BEYOND BLACK THURSDAY

Second Schweinfurt was one of the three worst days in the combat history of the 306th Group, and its personnel were stunned. The losses aside, however, the damage to Schweinfurt was greater than in the first raid and, under ideal circumstances, had the raids been continued, the German ball-bearing industry would have been severely affected. After Second Schweinfurt, and the destruction of sixty-seven percent of the ball-bearing production, Albert Speer concluded that German war potential was near total disaster, but "what really saved us was the fact that from this time on the enemy to our astonishment once again ceased his attacks on the ball-bearing industry."[1] The truth is, it was impossible to resume attacking anything other than "easy" targets, where the bombers could be escorted by short-range fighters, until the Eighth Air Force rebuilt its forces in the following month.

The ten air crews the 306th lost on Second Schweinfurt were replaced later in October, by which time twelve new B-17s had been flown in and were awaiting them. Aircraft production in the United States was accelerating, and from this time on crews and planes would arrive as necessary to replace missing crews and lost or damaged Fortresses.

The seventy-nine raids in which the 306th participated that preceded Second Schweinfurt were only a beginning in its roster of targets—261 missions still remained for them to fly, three-quarters of their total of 341 combat operations. Halfway into the thirty months that the 306th was to be in active combat, the unit had lost eighty-seven Fortresses in the one hundred raids they had flown—seventy-four percent of the total losses they were to sustain in action. These losses averaged 5.8 aircraft a month; that is, the expenditure of nearly a six-plane squadron every thirty days. Another thirty aircraft would be lost in the next 141 missions in the final fifteen months of combat—a more comfortable average of two Fortresses a month.

This decrease in losses represents a major change in the nature of the air war over Germany: the introduction of the long-range P-51 fighter escort. The necessity for such escorts had been forcibly underscored by the losses on First Schweinfurt, and further demonstrated by the unsustainable drain on the Eighth Air Force on Black Thursday. In the face of a determined Luftwaffe capable of hurling hundreds of fighters against the bombers, the lacerating attacks and unacceptable losses over the Continent would continue. A fighter was needed that could accompany the bomb groups all the way to the target and and return with them.

Even as Second Schweinfurt was being flown, however, the North American P-51 Mustang was in production in the United States, a fighter that was capable of shielding the bombers from enemy fighters all the way to Berlin and back. These life-saving escorts began leaving the United States and touching down at their English bases to join the air war over Europe in November 1943. They entered combat quickly, on December 1. From that time on, they arrived in large numbers and their losses were promptly replaced. They quickly became the most numerous fighter in the Eighth Fighter Command in England.

Fighter pilots on both sides of the English Channel later agreed that the Mustang was the finest conventional fighter of the war, and it turned the tide of losses for the Eighth Air Force and gradually won air superiority over the Luftwaffe—a goal that was not realized until a full year after Second Schweinfurt. With the arrival of these superb aircraft the bombers no longer had to wave farewell when their "Little Friends," low on fuel, turned homeward as their formations entered German airspace. The swarms of German fighters that once had a single mission—destroy the bombers—now had to face the formidable swarms of Mustangs that chaperoned the invading forces. Attacking the bombers was risky enough, but they now had to keep a sharp lookout behind them to remain in the air, if they in fact were able to fight their way into the bomber stream.

With the Mustangs' appearance in German skies, Luftwaffe personnel from Göring to the operational fighter pilot began to sense that a new and decisive factor had been entered in the ledger against them. When the lack of fuel eventually grounded the German fighters, the Mustangs left the bombers unattended and attacked any strategic target that presented itself: bridges, locomotives, river barges, military convoys, and even the grounded aircraft of the Luftwaffe itself, destroying immobilized enemy fighters on the ground.

*   *   *

In the thirty months the 306th was in action, ground crews at Thurleigh[2] were to wait in vain for the return of 117 B-17s and the 1,170 men aboard them—Fortresses that never returned to their hardstands after a mission over the Continent. Ground crews for the missing bombers retired quietly to their quarters as jubilant members of the crews of the returning bombers welcomed their men—and ship—back to Station 111. The ground crews watched as fresh aircrews arrived, month after month, to either become veterans or vanish, sometimes after a single mission. Sometimes one of the "ground pounders" was smuggled aboard to fly a combat mission, but their role was to maintain the airworthiness of the Fortresses and sweat out the missions back in England.

As a thank-you gesture to ground crews and staff, special flights were scheduled in the latter part of May 1945 to carry these men over the group's recent targets in Europe. Flying at low

altitudes revealed to them, and indeed to many of the flyers
themselves for the first time, the extent of destruction they and their
comrades had imposed on Germany and occupied Europe. It was
an awesome sight to overfly the target cities and witness mile after
mile of shattered and burned-out buildings.

This destruction came at great cost, for group losses were high.
The 306th group historian, Russell Strong, concluded that 738 men
were killed in action, and that an even greater number, 885 men,
became prisoners of war. That is, one had a little better than 50
percent chance of surviving being shot down over the Continent,
although many of those survivors would be injured to one degree
or another. At one point there were said to be as many 306th officers
imprisoned at Stalag Luft III at Sagan, Germany—famed as the
locale of the "Great Escape"—as there were back at the base in
England.

The 306th earned many wartime awards, among them the only
Congressional Medal of Honor bestowed in the Eighth Air Force,
to Sgt. Maynard H. ("Snuffy") Smith; seven Distinguished Service
Crosses; 1,511 Distinguished Flying Crosses; 14,094 Air Medals; and
447 Purple Hearts. Still more Purple Hearts were posthumously
awarded to those crewmen killed in combat. Other honors included
a Distinguished Unit Citation to the "Fightin' Bitin' " 369th Bomb
Squadron on February 14—Valentine's Day!—1944, the only such
citation for a 306th unit during its wartime service.

Mission succeeded mission as the months passed, the targets
of varying recognition to today's reader. Familiar names include
Berlin, Frankfurt, Hamburg, Munich, Wilhelmshaven, Cologne,
Peenemunde, Schweinfurt (two more raids), and Kiel, as well as
missions to occasional targets in France and Belgium before their
liberation.

The continuing buildup in the Eighth Air Force inventory
permitted larger formations to be flown than in the past. In May
1944 the 306th began putting up more aircraft for each mission:
thirty to thirty-five aircraft were being flown instead of the eighteen
in earlier months. Flak was becoming more intense over major

targets, although fighter attacks were down. Indeed, during the summer many Fortresses began flying with only one waist gunner. There also was a change in pace for a week and a half in early June 1944, when the group's efforts were diverted to support missions for the Normandy campaign following D-Day. They reverted to the routine of strategic targets on June 18 when General Eisenhower released the Eighth Air Force from these tactical duties.

The last 306th plane to be shot down was *Flak Shack*, a 369th Squadron plane lost to Flak on April 10, 1945, on a mission to Oranienburg. The last operational mission by the 306th—number 341— was on April 19, 1945, with a raid on the marshalling yards at Falkenburg, near Berlin. After the devastating losses earlier in the war, the entry in the 367th Squadron history stating that "No E/A were seen and P51s gave close support throughout the mission" would bring an envious, wistful smile to the face of those who had survived those initial raids, particularly in late 1943, when the B-17s were flying unescorted.

*   *   *

The Eighth Air Force air bases in England today are stilled. The last heavy bombers and their fighter escorts thundered into the English skies a half-century ago, climbing above the clouds to assemble for their strikes against German industry. Grass now grows on the runways of most of the old bases, and at others farmers soon began to reclaim the land that had been theirs before the war. The few buildings that have not been put to use by local farmers as storage sheds or barns are now gone, or in ruins, their shattered windows admitting the rain.

Not all the air bases were deactivated quickly. At two of them, the homes of the 305th and 306th Bomb Groups, the men participated in a postwar program known as "Project Casey Jones."[3] These two groups were chosen because they were among those that had the longest records of service in the Eighth Air Force. Because of the aerial stability of the B-17, the old warbirds were chosen to be used as aerial camera platforms, and were stripped of their wartime accessories and fitted with aerial cameras. Flying carefully programmed parallel flights at four-mile intervals over much of western Europe and northern Africa, including Iceland and Greenland, their cameras snapped thousands of overlapping aerial photographs. When these images were pieced together, they provided a new and more accurate map of more than two million square miles of the Old World, the largest aerial mapping project then undertaken. Eventually, however, these photomapping bases also closed. At the conclusion of the project, the remaining B-17s were destroyed by setting explosive charges in them and blowing their tails off, after which they were junked.

The RAF did, of course, retain some of the bases. At Thurleigh, the ghosts remain, but they are not alone with their memories: a vibrant modern aerospace complex, the most advanced aviation research center in Europe, occupies the old air base, now renamed Bedford. After the war the base was occupied by the Royal Aircraft Establishment (RAE), a unit of the Ministry of Defense. A new 10,000-foot runway was built across those that launched the B-17s against Fortress Europe, one long enough to accommodate the new and faster jet aircraft. The first conventional flight trials of the forerunner of the Harrier fighter were at Bedford in February 1961, and early experimental flights of the Concorde were also made there. Returning 306th veterans must today obtain passes to enter their old base. Many of them have done so at reunions, but few men could now recognize their old home.

During wartime about 35,000 servicemen were stationed at Thurleigh. Today they are scattered over the globe, but there is a strong bond among these men who, when they were still little more than boys, entered what was for a majority of them the most exciting and dangerous time of their lives. They take deep pride in having carried out a difficult mission, but they do not glorify war. They saw too many of their friends' planes destroyed, and too many empty bunks on too many consecutive mornings after heavy losses over Europe. They are patriots, not zealots, and despite the visible and invisible scars they still carry from those bitter engagements, they have the satisfaction of having been part of a powerful instrument that was so important in the destruction of Nazi war potential.

Appendix

Researching the military career and combat experience of any individual soldier entails consulting a wide variety of unpublished as well as published sources. This appendix provides a list of those archives and veterans associations that supplied important material used in writing this book. It is not exhaustive, but it represents the kinds of material available to the public.

ARCHIVAL SOURCES

FILE 201. A veteran's service record is known as the 201 File. The National Personnel Records Center (NPRC) in St. Louis is the repository for United States Army officers separated after June 30, 1917, and enlisted personnel after October 31, 1912—as well as for the U.S. Air Force, Navy, Marine Corps, and Coast Guard for dates as early as 1864. The records, however, are not complete. On July 12, 1973, a fire destroyed about eighty percent of the records for United States Army personnel discharged between November 1, 1912, and January 1, 1960. Some of these records may be reconstructed from alternate sources in St. Louis and other locations, but this is a time-consuming process—when it is in fact possible. Some files simply cannot be reconstructed, as in the case of Elbert S. Wood. The release of information from a veteran's military record normally requires the written consent (signature) of the individual whose records are involved. Although the Privacy Act of 1974 does not apply to records of deceased individuals, Department of Defense instructions are that the NPRC must have the written consent of the next of kin if the subject is deceased. For purpose of release, the next of kin is defined as an unremarried widow or widower, son, daughter, father, mother, brother, or sister.

Military Personnel Records Center
9700 Page Boulevard
St. Louis, Missouri 63132

FILE 293. An Individual Deceased Personnel File, File 293, was prepared for all servicemen who died overseas, whether their remains were returned to the United States or buried in permanent military cemeteries abroad. These files also were prepared for individuals who were reported missing in action, since all such members of the military eventually were declared legally dead. Copies of the file may be obtained by members of the individual's immediate family from:

> Department of the Army
> U.S. Army Military Personnel Center
> Mortuary Affairs and Casualty Support Division
> 2461 Eisenhower Avenue
> Alexandria, Virginia 22331

FEDERAL RECORD CENTER, SUITLAND. Most Eighth Air Force archives are housed at this center in Maryland, just east of Washington, DC, although its mailing address is Washington, DC. Suitland is a repository for original Mission Reports, Combat Operations, Bombing Narratives, Intelligence Interrogations, Missing Air Crew Reports (MACR), and German reports on downed Allied aircraft (the *Luftgaukommando* records of the Luftwaffe). Tactical Mission Reports are also available on 16-millimeter microfilm at the Albert F. Simpson Historical Research Center in Alabama (see below).

During World War II the U.S. Army Air Forces required its group organizations to report within two days the names of any members of an air crew who did not return from a combat mission. They were also to provide details about the mission, the missing air crew member(s), and the aircraft. The Missing Air Crew Reports (sometimes called Missing Air Craft Reports) are today in the National Archives, and are available on microfiche at nominal cost. These records are open to any interested party.

> Modern Military Field Branch
> Military Archives Division
> National Archives
> Washington National Records Center Building
> Washington, DC 20409

THE UNITED STATES AIR FORCE HISTORICAL RESEARCH CENTER. This unit of the United States Air Force is the repository for Air Force historical documents. Most of the collection for World War II is on 16-millimeter microfilm, copies of which are also to be found in the National Archives at the Suitland Federal Record Center and at the Office of Air Force History, Bolling Air Force Base, Washington, DC. Unit histories, including group and squadron war diaries, provide coverage for the major commands, numbered air forces, and other subordinate units for Air Force activities beginning in 1942.

> United States Air Force
> Albert F. Simpson Historical Research Center
> Maxwell Air Force Base, Alabama 36112

VETERANS ADMINISTRATION. If you wish to get in touch with a veteran, you may write him in care of the regional office of the Veterans Administration. In a separate letter to the VA, tell what you can of his name, rank, serial number, and war record. Enclose your letter to him in a stamped envelope bearing his name and serial number. If the veteran is still alive, the letter will be forwarded to him; if he is not, your letter will be returned with the date of his death. This is all the information you will be able to obtain. Your letter will not be forwarded to his next of kin and, because of the Privacy Act of 1974, you will not be given the last known address of either the veteran or of the next of kin.

VETERANS ASSOCIATIONS

EIGHTH AIR FORCE HISTORICAL SOCIETY. For general information on Eighth Air Force veterans' groups, consult the *8th AF News*, a journal published quarterly by veterans of that unit. At periodic intervals this publication carries the names and addresses of contact agents for active Eighth Air Force bomb group associations. The *News* also publishes letters by those seeking information on former members. The society provides its more than 16,000 members with its quarterly journal, and maintains the 8th AF Clearinghouse. Reunions are held every year at different cities in the United States. Eighth Air Force servicemen, past and present, are invited to become members. Family members and others interested in furthering the aims of the society may join as associate members.

> Eighth Air Force Historical Society
> 711 South Smith Avenue
> St. Paul, Minnesota 55107

OTHER SOCIETIES. Many bomb groups have their own individual associations, the names and addresses for which appear from time to time in the *8th AF News*. Veterans of the 306th Bomb Group have an active organization and publish a quarterly newsletter, *306th Echoes*. Reunions are held annually. Documents about its history are being accumulated for donation to the U.S. Air Force Academy archives, Colorado Springs, Colorado.

Survivors of the October 14, 1943, mission to Schweinfurt have formed their own society, the Second Schweinfurt Memorial Association (S.S.M.A.). The group publishes *Briefing Report*, a quarterly newsletter, and holds a reunion every other (odd-numbered) year. For the current address of this organization, consult the listing of "Organizations Related to the 8th AF" in a recent issue of the *8th AF News*.

There are also several prisoner-of-war associations, many of them for the individual camps in which the serviceman was held captive. Most captured Eighth Air Force enlisted men were sent to Stalag XVII-B, near Krems, in northeastern Austria. Its former occupants have formed the "American Former Prisoners of War: Stalag XVII-B Association." Air Force officers were sent to various camps, but primarily to Stalag Luft III, near Sagan, Germany. The *Kriege Klarion* is a newsletter issued by the "Stalag Luft III Former Prisoners of War Association." Other camps for airmen included Stalag Luft I, IV, and VI. Addresses for these associations also are published periodically in *8th AF News*.

Notes

INTRODUCTION

1. Such constructions of past events are known today as "oral history," popularized by the works of such writers as Studs Terkel. Oral history, however, is not "history" as such unless it is subjected to careful, internal criticism. Differing recollections by eyewitnesses have been winnowed here to produce the most reliable story—but one that is nevertheless subject to error.

2. Paul D. Gray, "The Human Record of Conflict: Individual Military Service and Medical Records," *Prologue: Quarterly of the National Archives*, Vol. 23 (3), 1991, pp. 306–13.

3. See Appendix: Veterans Administration.

CHAPTER ONE

1. Evelyn Boyd and Eric Munday, "The Missing Research and Enquiry Service," *Air Clues*, Vol. 40 (5), 1986, pp. 187–90.

2. More technical information is available in the "Report on RAF and Dominions Air Force Missing Research and Enquiry Service 1944–1949," Reference AIR 55/65, London: Public Record Office.

CHAPTER TWO

1. Kenneth P. Werrell, "The Strategic Bombing of Germany in World War II: Costs and Accomplishments," *Journal of American History*, Vol. 73 (3), 1986, pp. 702–13. A concise history of the topic by a strategic bombing authority.

2. Adolf Galland, *The First and the Last*, New York: Henry Holt, 1954, p. 185. This book, by the Luftwaffe's General of the Fighters, was one of the first studies to recount the air war from the German point of view. It is still

a basic and very readable account, both from an operational and strategic point of view.

3. Albert Speer, *Spandau: The Secret Diaries*, New York: Macmillan, 1976, p. 375.

4. R. J. Overy, *The Air War: 1939–1945*, New York: Stein and Day, 1980, p. 158. This general view of the aims and accomplishments of the air war, worldwide, has an excellent bibliography.

CHAPTER THREE

1. Roger A. Freeman, *Mighty Eighth War Manual*, London: Jane's, 1984, pp. 271, 313. Freeman provides an overview of the aircraft, operations, armament, and installations of the Eighth Air Force. As the acknowledged authority on that force, Freeman's many books furnish an exhaustive treatment of this service. They are lavishly illustrated.

2. Arthur P. Bove, *First Over Germany: 306th Bombardment Group in World War II*, San Angelo, TX: Newsphoto Publishing, 1946. The first history to appear of the 306th Bomb Group, Bove's is augmented and superseded by Strong, 1982.

3. Ibid., p. 6.

4. Budd J. Peaslee, *Heritage of Valor: The Eighth Air Force in World War II*, Philadelphia: Lippincott, 1964, p. 151. Peaslee, commander of the First Air Division of Second Schweinfurt, was a founder and past president of the Second Schweinfurt Memorial Association, established in 1975 to bring together the surviving members of mission number 115.

5. Herbert Molloy Mason, Jr., *The Rise of the Luftwaffe*, New York: Ballantine, 1973, pp. 140–42.

6. Alfred Price, *Luftwaffe: Birth, Life and Death of an Air Force*, New York: Ballantine, 1969, pp. 10–13.

7. Ibid., p. 26.

8. Cajus Bekker, *The Luftwaffe War Diaries*, London: Macdonald, 1966; New York: Ballantine, 1969, pp. 84–96, 116. A comprehensive account of the Luftwaffe in World War II, based on official German sources and personal narrations by its members. A standard source.

CHAPTER FOUR

1. Cajus Bekker, *The Luftwaffe War Diaries*, London: Macdonald, 1966; New York: Ballantine, 1969, p. 471.

2. Ralph N. Phillips, "Navigation Problems in England," *Air Force*, Vol. 27 (6), 1944, p. 36.

3. Tactical Mission Reports, p. 311; Montgomery, AL: United States Air Force Historical Research Center.

CHAPTER FIVE

1. John H. Woolnough, "The Clark Gable Story," *8th AF News*, Vol. 8 (3), 1982, p. 8. Clark Gable starred in a 1948 MGM motion picture, *Command Decision*, playing the role of an Eighth Air Force commander sending his planes on strategic missions to "Schweinhafen," a fictional German town apparently inspired by the Schweinfurt raids.

2. Roger A. Freeman, *The Mighty Eighth: Units, Men and Machines: A History of the U.S. 8th Army Air Force*, London: Macdonald; Garden City, NY: Doubleday, 1970, p. 73.

3. ——. *Mighty Eighth War Manual*, London: Jane's, 1984, p. 118.

4. Ibid., p. 73.

5. Max Hastings, *Bomber Command*, New York: Touchstone, 1989, p. 214. This unofficial account of the development and execution of the British area-bombing offensive against Germany is a compelling story by a first-rate author.

CHAPTER SIX

1. Elmer Bendiner, *The Fall of Fortresses*, New York: G. P. Putnam's Sons, 1980, p. 1. Bendiner, a navigator with the 379th Bomb Group, and a participant in Second Schweinfurt, provides a personal and gripping narrative of air battles, with his own cogent observations on command, tactics, and strategy.

2. Cajus Bekker, *The Luftwaffe War Diaries*, London: Macdonald, 1966; New York: Ballantine, 1969, p. 506.

3. Martin Middlebrook, *The Schweinfurt-Regensburg Mission*, London: Allen Lane, 1983; New York: Scribners, 1983, p. 28. This book explores the events of First Schweinfurt in detail. It is based on official accounts and on recollections by 300 of its participants.

4. Martin Caidin, *Black Thursday*, New York: E. P. Dutton, 1960, p. 165. The definitive but unofficial account of Second Schweinfurt.

5. Robert E. O'Hearn, ed., *In My Book You're All Heroes*, Bakersfield, CA: Hall Letter Shop, 1984, p. 109. The seventy-eight vignettes in this anthology—all by survivors of Second Schweinfurt—cover many aspects of mission number 115.

6. Ibid., pp. 83–84.

7. Adolf Galland, *The First and the Last*, New York: Henry Holt, 1954, p. 140.

8. Capt. John R. McCrary and David E. Scherman, *First of the Many*, New York: Simon and Schuster, 1944, p. 214. This is a personal account of Eighth Air Force life in Britain—on base, on leave, and in the air, with many fine photographs by *Life* magazine photographer Scherman.

9. Galland, p. 180.

CHAPTER SEVEN

1. Most of the details of the Second Schweinfurt mission are from the 306th War Diary and the 369th War Diary, as well as Tactical Mission Reports.

2. Russell A. Strong, *First Over Germany: A History of the 306th Bombardment Group*, Winston-Salem, NC: Hunter Publishing, 1982, p. 151. Strong's book details the history of the 306th Bomb Group, mission by mission. Insofar as is practical, the fate of each aircraft lost and its crew is given.

3. Biographical details for Herbert Schob are taken from: Werner Girbig's letter to the author of October 18, 1987; Holger Nauroth and Werner Held, *Messerschmitt Bf110: Zerstörer an allen Fronten, 1939–1945*, Stuttgart: Motorbuch Verlag, 1978 (this illustrated history of the Bf-110 Destroyer uses many photos provided by Schob showing him throughout his Luftwaffe career); Raymond L. Proctor, *Hitler's Luftwaffe in the Spanish Civil War*, Contributions in Military History No. 35, Westport, CT: Greenwood Press, 1983, pp. 233, 262; and Raymond F. Toliver and Trevor J. Constable, *Fighter Aces of the Luftwaffe*, New York: Macmillan, 1968 (reprinted in 1979 by Ballantine as *Horrido!*), p. 324.

4. Earl H. Beck, *Under the Bombs: The German Home Front, 1942–1945*, Lexington: University Press of Kentucky, 1986, p. 72.

5. Martin Caidin, *The Night Hamburg Died*, New York: Ballantine, 1960. This is the most readable account of Operation GOMORRAH, although the description of German civilians being shot to put them out of their misery is disputed.

CHAPTER EIGHT

1. Missing Air Crew Report No. 821, Federal Records Center, Modern Military Field Branch, Suitland, MD.

2. Alois Stadtmüller, *Maingebiet und Spessart im Zweiten Weltkrieg*, Aschaffenburg, Germany: Geschichts-und Kunstverein Aschaffenburg e.V., 1982, pp. 177–78. *The Districts of Main and Spessart in World War II* is an objective overview of the Second World War, focusing on the air war and defeat of Germany, 1939–1945. Founded on documents, it is augmented by many eyewitness accounts.

3. Hans-Heiri Stapfer, *Strangers in a Strange Land*, Carrollton, TX: Squadron/Signal Publications, 1988, pp. 17–19, 49–54.

4. Cliff T. Bishop, *Fortresses of the Big Triangle First*, Guildford, Eng.: East Anglia Books, 1986, p. 177; and Roger A. Freeman, *Mighty Eighth War Manual*, London: Jane's, 1984, p. 157.

5. Leland A. Dowden, *One and One Half Missions*, San Mateo, CA: Western Book/Journal Press, 1989.

CHAPTER NINE

1. This chapter is compiled primarily from information in Lieutenant Wood's 293 file, interwoven with on-the-site interviews with numerous German eyewitnesses, all of them thanked in the Acknowledgments.

2. Leo V. Bishop, Frank J. Glasgow, and George A. Fisher, *The Fighting Forty-Fifth*, Baton Rouge, LA: Army and Navy Publishing Co., 1946, pp. 160–66. This unit history of the 45th Infantry Division, Seventh Army, gives a brief account of the capture of Aschaffenburg on April 3.

3. Thomas J. Howard, *The 106th Cavalry Group in Europe, 1945–1946*, Augsburg, Germany: J. P. Himmer KG, 1945, p. 110. The author of this history of the 106th Cavalry, Seventh Army, provides a day-to-day account of their advance from Normandy to central Germany.

4. Alois Stadtmüller, *Maingebiet und Spessart im Zweiten Weltkrieg*, Aschaffenburg: Geschichts-und Kunstverein Aschaffenburg e.V., 1982, pp. 375, 382–83.

5. Capt. Eric Friedham, "Beneath the Rubble of Schweinfurt," *Air Force*, Vol. 28 (6), 1945, pp. 4–6, 61.

6. Earl F. Ziemke, *The U.S. Army in the Occupation of Germany, 1944–1946*, Washington, DC: Center of Military History, United States Army, 1975, p. 380.

CHAPTER TEN

1. W. Raymond Wood and Lori Ann Stanley, "Recovery and Identification of World War II Dead: American Graves Registration Activities in Europe," *Journal of Forensic Sciences*, Vol. 34 (6), 1989, pp. 1365–73; and

Edward Steere and Thayer M. Boardman, *Final Disposition of World War II Dead: 1945–51*, Historical Studies, Series II, No. 4, Washington, DC: Office of the Quartermaster General, 1957, pp. 1–14.

Wood and Stanley's summary of the AGRC activities in Europe uses the example of Lieutenant Wood as a case study in forensic anthropology. Steere and Boardman, as well as Steere (below), are the definitive accounts of the activities of the AGRC worldwide in World War II.

2. Edward Steere, *The Graves Registration Service in World War II*, Historical Studies, No. 21, Washington, DC: Office of the Quartermaster General, Government Printing Office, 1951, pp. 28, 93, 98.

3. Steere and Boardman, pp. 239–72.

4. Ibid., pp. 165, 171–73, 183–88, 272, 613.

5. Harry L. Shapiro, in a letter to the author, November 4, 1987.

6. Professor Simonin, *"Identification des corps des soldats américains inconnus,"* *Acta Medicinae Legalis et Socialis*, Vol. 1 (1), 1948, pp. 382–86;

Steere and Boardman, pp. 617–25; and F. Vandervael, *"L'Identification anthropologique des morts inconnus de la guerre dans l'armée américaine,"* *Revue Médicale de Liège,* Vol. 8 (19), 1953, pp. 617–21.

CHAPTER ELEVEN

1. This entire chapter is based on Lieutenant Wood's 293 file and indicates to the reader the massive wealth of detail the government maintains on behalf of casualties.

2. Edward Steere and Thayer M. Boardman, *Final Disposition of World War II Dead: 1945–51,* Historical Studies, Series II, No. 4, Washington, DC: Office of the Quartermaster General, 1957, p. 341.

CHAPTER TWELVE

1. Albert Speer, *Inside the Third Reich,* New York: Macmillan, 1970, pp. 372–73.

2. Russell A. Strong, *First Over Germany: A History of the 306th Bombardment Group,* Winston-Salem, NC: Hunter Publishing, 1982.

3. Robert J. Boyd, *Project "Casey Jones," 1945–1946,* Offutt Air Force Base, Nebraska: Office of the Historian, Headquarters Strategic Air Command, 1988.

References and Sources

ARCHIVAL SOURCES

Federal Records Center, Modern Military Field Branch, Suitland, MD:
   Missing Air Crew Reports, Nos. 819–821
   Mission Reports for 306th Bomb Group, September 2 to November 23,
      1943; Record Group 18, Boxes 633–34, and 637
   Operations Narratives, 306th Bomb Group, Record Group 18, Entry
      7,T906–908, for August 19, 1943, to December 13, 1943
   World War II Operations Reports, 1940–1948, The Adjutant General's
      Office, European Theater, 97-AGRC-0.1, Vols. 1–6, 1945 to 1949,
      Record Group 94, Boxes 284–87

United States Air Force Historical Research Center, Montgomery, AL:
   Unit histories ("War Diaries") for the 306th Bomb Group and the 369th
      Bomb Squadron
   Tactical Mission Reports for August 31 to November 18, 1943 (Microfilm
      Roll No. A5915); and for October 9 to October 25, 1943 (Microfilm
      Roll No. A5942)

United States Army Military Personnel Center, Mortuary Affairs and Casualty
Support Division, Alexandria, VA:
   Individual Deceased Personnel File 293 for 2nd Lieutenant Elbert S.
      Wood

Archives of Stadt Alzenau in Unterfranken, Bavaria, Germany:
   Death certificate of Elbert S. Wood

Public Record Office, London:
   Report on the RAF and Dominions Air Force Missing Research and
      Enquiry Service 1944–1945. Reference AIR 55/65.

Donald Earl Williams, Hereford, Arizona:
   Prisoner of war diary

PUBLISHED SOURCES

Aschaffenburg *Main-Echo*. Articles appearing in the April 23, July 18, and December 22, 1987, and the February 24, 1988, issues in the *"Alzenau und Kahlgrund"* section.

Barker, A. J. *German Infantry Weapons of World War II*. London: Arms and Armour Press; New York: Arco Publishing, 1969.

Beck, Earl H. *Under the Bombs: The German Home Front, 1942–1945*. Lexington: University Press of Kentucky, 1986.

Bekker, Cajus. *The Luftwaffe War Diaries*. London: Macdonald, 1966; New York: Ballantine, 1969.

Bendiner, Elmer. *The Fall of Fortresses*. New York: G. P. Putnam's Sons, 1980.

Bevans, Charles I. *Treaties and Other International Agreements of the United States of America, 1776–1949*. Washington, DC: Department of State Publication 8441, 1969.

Bishop, Cliff T. *Fortresses of the Big Triangle First*. Guildford, Eng.: East Anglia Books, 1986.

Bishop, Leo V., Frank J. Glasgow, and George A. Fisher. *The Fighting Forty-Fifth*. Baton Rouge: Army and Navy Publishing Company, 1946.

Bowman, Martin W. *Home by Christmas? The Story of US 8th/15th Air Force Airmen at War*. Wellingborough, Northamptonshire, Eng.: Patrick Stephens, 1987.

Bove, Arthur P. *First Over Germany: 306th Bombardment Group in World War II*. San Angelo, TX: Newsfoto Publishing Co., 1946.

Boyd, Evelyn, and Eric Munday. "The Missing Research and Enquiry Service." *Air Clues*, Vol. 40 (5), 1986, pp. 187–90.

Boyd, Robert J. *Project "Casey Jones," 1945–1946*. Offutt Air Force Base, Nebraska: Office of the Historian, Headquarters Strategic Air Command, 1988.

Caidin, Martin. *Black Thursday*. New York: E. P. Dutton, 1960.

——. *The Night Hamburg Died*. New York: Ballantine, 1960.

Coffey, Thomas M. *Decision Over Schweinfurt: The U.S. 8th Air Force Battle for Daylight Bombing*. New York: David McKay, 1977.

Craven, Frank W., and James L. Cate. *The Army Air Forces in World War II*, Vols. 1–3. Chicago: University of Chicago Press, 1948–51.

Daniels, Gordon, ed. *A Guide to the Reports of the United States Strategic Bombing Survey*, Vol. 1: *Europe*. Guides and Handbooks, Supplementary Series No. 2. London: Offices of the Royal Historical Society, 1981.

Dowden, Leland A. *One and One Half Missions*. San Mateo, CA: Western Book/Journal Press, 1989.

Ellis, L. F., and A. E. Warhurst. *Victory in the West*, Vol. 2: *The Defeat of*

Germany. London: Her Majesty's Stationery Office, 1968.

Foy, David A. *For You the War Is Over*. New York: Stein and Day, 1984.

Frazer, Maj. Charles D. "Battle Conditioning in the U.K." *Air Force*, Vol. 27 (4), 1944, pp. 22–24.

Freeman, Roger A. *The Mighty Eighth: Units, Men and Machines: A History of the U.S. 8th Army Air Force*. London: Macdonald; Garden City: Doubleday, 1970.

——. *B-17 Fortress at War*. Shepperton, Eng.: Ian Allan; New York: Scribners, 1977.

——. *Airfields of the Eighth*. London: Battle of Britain Prints International, 1978.

——. *Mighty Eighth War Diary*. London: Jane's, 1981.

——. *Mighty Eighth War Manual*. London: Jane's, 1984.

Friedham, Capt. Eric. "Beneath the Rubble of Schweinfurt." *Air Force*, Vol. 28 (6), 1945, pp. 4–6, 61.

Galland, Adolf. *The First and the Last*. New York: Henry Holt, 1954.

Gotts, Steve. "Artwork of the Eighth." *After the Battle*, Vol. 8 (30), 1980, pp. 47–53.

Gray, Paul D. "The Human Record of Conflict: Individual Military Service and Medical Records." *Prologue, Quarterly of the National Archives*, Vol. 23 (3), 1991, pp. 306–13.

Greenfield, Kent Roberts. *American Strategy in World War II: A Reconsideration*. Malabar, FL: Robert E. Krieger Publishing, 1982.

Hastings, Max. *Bomber Command*. New York: Touchstone, 1989.

Herbert, Col. George F. "Army Personnel Missing in Action." *Prisoners of War Bulletin*, Vol. 2 (3), 1944, pp. 4–5.

——. "Determining the Fate of Army Personnel Missing in Action." *Prisoners of War Bulletin*, Vol. 2 (12), 1944, pp. 6–7.

Howard, Thomas J. *The 106th Cavalry Group in Europe, 1944–1945*. Augsburg, Germany: J. P. Himmer KG, 1945.

Jablonsky, Edward. *Flying Fortress: The Illustrated Biography of the B-17s and the Men Who Flew Them*. New York: Doubleday, 1965.

Kaplan, Philip, and Rex Alan Smith. *One Last Look: A Sentimental Journey to the Eighth Air Force Heavy Bomber Bases of World War II in England*. New York: Abbeville Press, 1983.

Kuhl, George C. *Wrong Place, Wrong Time*. Atglen, PA.: Schiffer Publishing, 1993.

Lay, Jr., Bierne, and Sy Bartlett. *Twelve O'Clock High!* New York: Harper's, 1948.

Leasure, William C. "Navigating Over Europe." *Air Force*, Vol. 26 (7), 1943, pp. 15–16.

McClendon, Dennis E. *The Lady Be Good*. New York: Stein and Day, 1962.

McCrary, Capt. John R., and David E. Scherman. *First of the Many*. New York: Simon and Schuster, 1944.

McDonald, Charles B. *The Last Offensive: United States Army in World War II, The European Theater of Operations*. Washington, DC: Office of the Chief of Military History, United States Army, 1973.

Mason, Jr., Herbert Molloy. *The Rise of the Luftwaffe*. New York: Ballantine, 1973.

Maurer, Maurer, ed. *World War II Combat Squadrons of the United States Air Force*. New York: Smithmark Publishers, 1992.

Middlebrook, Martin. *The Schweinfurt-Regensburg Mission*. London: Allen Lane, 1983; New York: Scribners, 1983.

Morrison, Wilbur H. *Fortress Without a Roof*. New York: St. Martin's Press, 1982.

Nauroth, Holger, and Werner Held. *Messerschmitt Bf110: Zerstörer an allen Fronten, 1939–1945*. Stuttgart: Motorbuch Verlag, 1978.

O'Hearn, Robert E., ed. *In My Book You're All Heroes*. Bakersfield, CA: Hall Letter Shop, 1984.

Overy, R. J. *The Air War, 1939–1945*. New York: Stein and Day, 1980.

Peaslee, Budd J. *Heritage of Valor: The Eighth Air Force in World War II*. Philadelphia: Lippincott, 1964.

Phillips, Ralph N. "Navigation Problems in England." *Air Force*, Vol. 27 (6), 1944, pp. 36–37.

Price, Alfred. *Luftwaffe: Birth, Life and Death of an Air Force*. New York: Ballantine, 1969.

——. *Battle Over the Reich*. London: Ian Allen; New York: Scribners, 1973.

——. *Luftwaffe Handbook, 1939–1945*. New York: Scribners, 1977.

Proctor, Raymond L. *Hitler's Luftwaffe in the Spanish Civil War*. Contributions in Military History No. 35. Westport, CT: Greenwood Press, 1983.

Sheehan, Susan. *A Lost Plane*. New York: G. P. Putnam's Sons, 1986.

Simonin, Professor. "*Identification des corps des soldats américains inconnus*." *Acta Medicinae Legalis et Socialis* Vol. 1 (1), 1948, pp. 382–86.

Snow, Charles E. "The Identification of the Unknown War Dead." *American Journal of Physical Anthropology* Vol. 6 (3), 1948, pp. 323–28.

Speer, Albert. *Inside the Third Reich*. New York: Macmillan, 1970.

——. *Spandau: The Secret Diaries*. New York: Macmillan, 1976.

Stadtmüller, Alois. *Maingebiet und Spessart im Zweiten Weltkrieg*. Aschaffenburg, Germany: Geschichts-und Kunstverein Aschaffenburg e.V., 1982.

Stapfer, Hans-Heiri. *Strangers in a Strange Land*. Carrollton, TX: Squadron/Signal, 1988.

Steere, Edward. *The Graves Registration Service in World War II.* Historical Studies, No. 21. Washington, DC: Office of the Quartermaster General, Government Printing Office, 1951.

Steere, Edward, and Thayer M. Boardman. *Final Disposition of World War II Dead: 1945–51.* Historical Studies, Series II, No. 4. Washington, DC: Office of the Quartermaster General, Government Printing Office, 1957.

Strong, Russell A. *First Over Germany: A History of the 306th Bombardment Group.* Winston-Salem, NC: Hunter Publishing, 1982.

Sweetman, John. *Schweinfurt: Disaster in the Skies.* Ballantine Campaign Book No. 17. New York: Ballantine, 1971.

Toliver, Raymond F., and Trevor J. Constable. *Fighter Aces of the Luftwaffe.* New York: Macmillan, 1968. (Reprinted as *Horrido!* New York: Bantam Books, 1979.)

United States Army Air Force. *Departure Point: Class Book of 43-9.* San Marcos, TX: Army Air Force Navigation School, San Marcos Air Field, 1943.

United States War Department. *Graves Registration: Technical Manual 10-630.* Washington, DC: Government Printing Office, 1941.

——. *Graves Registration Service: Permanent Interment of World War II Dead.* Special Regulations No. 830-110-5. Washington, DC: Government Printing Office, 1949.

Vandervael, F. *"L'Identification anthropologique des morts inconnus de la guerre dans l'armée américaine." Revue Médicale de Liège*, Vol. 8 (19), 1953, pp. 617-21.

Werrell, Kenneth P. "The Strategic Bombing of Germany in World War II: Costs and Accomplishments." *Journal of American History*, Vol. 73 (3), 1986, pp. 702-13.

Williams, Mary H. *Chronology: 1941–1945.* United States Army in World War II, Special Studies. Washington, DC: Center of Military History, United States Army, 1960.

Wood, W. Raymond, and Lori Ann Stanley. "Recovery and Identification of World War II Dead: American Graves Registration Activities in Europe." *Journal of Forensic Sciences*, Vol. 34 (6), 1989, pp. 1365-73.

Woolnough, John H. "The Clark Gable Story." *8th AF News*, Vol. 8 (3), 1982, p. 8.

Ziemke, Earl F. *The U.S. Army in the Occupation of Germany, 1944–1946.* Washington, DC: Center of Military History, United States Army, 1975.

Index